ACTION!

THE NEW MEDITATION CODE

**80% of All Men & Women Meditate
Without Sitting Like a Monk!
Meditation is Now Action!
Four Zones, 40 Ways
Sports-Fitness, Creative Activities
Social Relations, Mindful Living**

Paul B Farrell, MRP, JD, PhD

©2018 Paul B. Farrell. All rights reserved.

No part of this book may be reproduced, stored in a retrieval system, or transmitted by any means without the written permission of the author.

ISBN-10: 0692056939
ISBN-13: 978-0-6920-5693-6

Printed in the United States of America

TABLE OF CONTENTS
THE NEW MEDITATION

INTRODUCTION
0.1 — Workplace Stress, Goals, Benefits & Solutions — ix
0.2 — Four Rules of All Meditation, Ancient and Modern — xi
0.3 — Three Reasons Sitting Meditation Gets The Media Spotlight — xv
0.4 — The Four Zones of the New Millionaire Meditation — xix
0.5 — A 10-Day Experiment—Find Out What Works For You — xxi

PART ONE: TRADITIONAL SITTING MEDITATION
THE MENTAL ZONE
1.1 — THE RELAXATION RESPONSE — 3
1.2 — BREATH COUNTING — 8
1.3 — MIND/BODY SCANNING — 12
1.4 — MANTRAS & CHANTING — 16
1.5 — MINDFULNESS & COMPASSION — 20
1.6 — POSITIVE AFFIRMATIONS — 25
1.7 — CENTERING PRAYER — 29
1.8 — INSPIRATIONAL READING — 33
1.9 — THE OFFICE BREAK — 38
2.0 — CAREER & LIFE PLANNING — 44

NEW WORLD OF MEDITATION

PART TWO
THE SPORTS/FITNESS ZONE
10 Ways to Meditate & Stay Physically Fit Too

2.1 — **RUNNING** as Meditation — 58
2.2 — **YOGA** as Meditation — 64
2.3 — **TENNIS** as Meditation — 69
2.4 — **GOLF** as Meditation — 75
2.5 — **WALKING, HIKING & CLIMBING** as Meditation — 80
2.6 — **THE MARTIAL ARTS** as Meditation — 85
2.7 — **TAI CHI** as Meditation — 90
2.8 — **SWIMMING & SURFING** as Meditation — 96
2.9 — **FLY FISHING** as Meditation — 100
3.0 — **GARDENING & DAILY LIVING** as Meditation — 104

PART THREE
THE CREATIVITY ZONE
10 Ways to Meditate with Passion & Enjoy Life!

3.1 — **CREATIVE VISUALIZATION** as Meditation	116
3.2 — **PERSONAL JOURNALS** as Meditation	121
3.3 — **CREATIVE WRITING** as Meditation	125
3.4 — **THE MUSICAL ARTS** as Meditation	129
3.5 — **DANCE** as Meditation	135
3.6 — **ACTING & THE PERFORMING ARTS** as Meditation	139
3.7 — **PAINTING & THE FINE ARTS** as Meditation	146
3.8 — **HOBBIES & CRAFTS** as Meditation	151
3.9 — **AN "ARTIST DATE"** as Meditation	158
4.0 — **THE ART of "DOING NOTHING"** as Meditation	164

PART FOUR
THE RELATIONSHIP ZONE
10 Ways to Meditate—Sharing Your Values

4.1 — **MASTERMINDS** as Meditation	171
4.2 — **LEADERSHIP** as Meditation	175
4.3 — **PUBLIC SERVICE** as Meditation	176
4.4 — **MENTORING & COACHING** as Meditation	177
4.5 — **SELF-HELP PROGRAMS** as Meditation	178
4.6 — **COUNSELING & THERAPY** as Meditation	179
4.7 — **RELIGIOUS CELEBRATIONS** as Meditation	180
4.8 — **PILGRIMAGES & JOURNEYS** as Meditation	180
4.9 — **INTIMATE RELATIONSHIPS** as Meditation	182
5.0 — **PARENTING** as Meditation	184

MORE READING	187

THIS IS THE ONLY BOOK ON MEDITATION YOU'LL EVER NEED ... AND HERE'S WHY

—In less that an hour you will learn everything you need to know about meditating, doing things you already enjoy doing, anytime and anywhere.

—You'll learn that millions of Americans are already meditating while doing what comes naturally to them—walking, hiking, cycling, running, swimming, tennis, golf, surfing, martial arts, plus creative activities like writing in personal journals, strolling through museums—and even eating chocolate can be meditation says America's leading heart specialist.

—You will also learn how millions of people are already meditating without sitting, burning incense, or chanting mantras, without relying on a guru, and without even calling what they're doing 'meditation.'

—You will quickly learn the four simple rules about everything you'll ever need to know to transform anything you do into a meditation—in your work, at play, with your friends and loved ones—and do it without sitting like a monk for hours. And these are the same basic rules that have been practiced by the great masters worldwide throughout history.

—You'll also see how many men and women quietly transform their work and personal lives into a way of meditating and living at peace with themselves, their families, friends and the world around them.

* * * * * * *

Now that I have your attention, please join me in discovering the benefits of this new way of life: stress reduction, a healthier happier life, physically, mentally and spiritually, more satisfying relationships at work and at home, increased energy, higher productivity, financial success, confidence, and peace of mind.

— Paul B. Farrell, JD, PhD

THE
NEW MEDITATION

FOR BUSY PEOPLE WHO JUST CAN'T "SIT STILL!"

The scene, a temple. Four young Zen monks sitting in meditation. Eyes closed. Legs crossed in the traditional za-zen position. Hands folded lightly in their laps. Fingers pointing to heaven. So peaceful. Serene. Well, that is, all of the young monks are peaceful except for one anxious beginner. Eyes darting. Fingers tapping. He has a cell phone propped at his ear. One hand muffles his whispered message: "It's not working!"

What's not working? The meditation? His training? The phone? No, the scene is actually a metaphor, a puzzle, a koan. His world is not working, it is a moving target. Today we are witness to an historic revolution. Everywhere, new pressures, stresses, increasing anxieties, inner turmoil. Our world is divided, our souls are in conflict. Thus we begin an exciting quest to become whole, to discover who we really are, to become authentic, the real you, to get rich in spirit, in fact, in love, to achieve our goals, to be happy, at peace, complete, to make your daily life a meditation.

INTRODUCTION

ASK ANYONE IN the business of stress management and they'll tell you that meditation is the best tool available in reducing stress, the number one health problem in Corporate America today. Stress drains $300 billion from the economy every year, in absenteeism, lower productivity, increased healthcare costs, a huge loss of talent. In fact, experts tell us 60-90 percent of all doctors' visits are the result of stress-related medical conditions, and meditation will reduce our stress.

So what's the problem? *Sitting meditation*—it doesn't work for most of today's busy Americans. And yet, sitting meditation techniques are the ones most frequently used in stress management. That's right, even though sitting meditation is not the best method of meditating for most people, it remains the favorite of gurus and the one most frequently spotlighted in the media.

THE NEW MEDITATION

SITTING DOESN'T WORK FOR 80% OF US
WE NEED NEW WAYS TO MEDITATE

More specifically: In my research for *The Millionaire Code,* a study of the wealth-building styles of the sixteen different personality types, it became quite apparent that sitting meditation works best for only about 20 percent of America's population. However, sitting is not the best way for the other 80 percent. Their personality types are more naturally suited to action-oriented meditations, rather than passive methods relying on mental techniques.

What does this mean for you? Simply this: *The odds are high—four out of five—that sitting meditation is not the best way for you, and you need another kind of meditation* if you want the benefits; stress reduction, physical health, increased energy, higher productivity, and success on the bottom line.

My guess is that you probably already know all this. You've already tried sitting meditation on the advice of a friend, a therapist, or after reading about it in the news. You tried *but you gave it up,* telling yourself that you just don't have the time, or it is just too darn boring, or you hate all that sitting. But I would also bet the real reason is that sitting meditation doesn't fit your personality type, and as a result, it just isn't the best way for you to meditate.

THE "NEW MEDITATION" CLUB
FOR PEOPLE WHO CAN'T SIT STILL

So join the club. There are millions like you, all searching for a way to meditate that fits their personality type and lifestyle, but most of all, feels right personally. Picking the right one is actually easy and simple, if you use the four simple rules outlined in this training manual.

This simple approach is different from any other meditation program you've ever read about or tried. There is no one-size-fits-all method you must do without fail, quite the opposite. While this approach uses elements common to ancient and contemporary meditation methods, the main goal is to help you find a new way of meditating that is uniquely your way.

INTRODUCTION

THE FOUR BASIC RULES OF ALL MEDITATIONS

When you get down to basics, there are only four very simple rules, and they apply to all meditations, secular and spiritual, ancient and contemporary, whether you're moving or sitting, alone or meditating in groups. These rules will work for anyone, anywhere, in any situation, at any time. *They will work for you.* These are the rules common to all methods of meditation and they will work no matter what specific activities you select for your meditation, period.

RULE ONE

FOCUS ON WHAT YOU'RE DOING IN THIS MOMENT, AND NOTHING ELSE!

All meditation techniques, from ancient times to the present, begin with this one fundamental rule: Whatever you are doing at this moment must be exactly what you are doing at this moment, and nothing else. No distractions.

Focus, concentrate, be aware and fully present of whatever you're doing right now—that's what meditation is all about. Whether you're working in the office, commuting, eating, dancing, reading, bowling, playing golf or tennis, practicing martial arts, singing or reading to a two-year-old child, if you stay completely in the moment, you are meditating. The great spiritual masters have been teaching us this core rule for centuries. It works.

RULE TWO

ANYTHING YOU DO CAN BE A MEDITATION—*ANYTHING*!

As long as you're focused on what you're doing in the moment, then anything you do can be a meditation. This simple principle—that anything can be a meditation—is not new. Experts from ancient spiritual masters to modern stress management clinicians all know this secret.

Throughout this book you'll see stories about men and women already experimenting with alternative ways of meditating—fly-fishing, surfing, tennis, golf, martial arts, woodworking, and journal writing—things they already do and enjoy. Meditation becomes part of your everyday life rather than an isolated ritual performed twenty minutes in the morning and in the evening.

RULE THREE

TRUST YOURSELF! THE RESULTS ARE WITHIN YOU

You are the sole judge of your meditation program: You experiment, pick what to do, where, when, how. You decide if it's working. What if it doesn't feel right? Trust yourself. You'll know. It's your decision. Period.

Only you can tell if what you're doing is right for you, whether you're getting results, whether it's time to try something else. No outside authorities, no gurus, monks, teachers or anyone out there, will ever know better than you what's best for you. There's only one right way, your way. Trust yourself.

INTRODUCTION

RULE FOUR

KEEP IT SIMPLE, EVERYONE MEDITATES
WE DO IT NATURALLY

There really is no big mysterious secret. Meditation is as simple and as natural as breathing. And yet many experts still make such a big deal of it. The truth is, you're already meditating, it just happens naturally. Most the time you do it without thinking you're meditating—and without calling it "meditation."

In fact, if there is a secret, the secret is that you can't "not meditate," that's impossible. Everybody does it, naturally. It just happens. We do it often during the day, in breathing, reading, listening to music, walking, praying, exercising, sports, affirming life goals, working on a positive mental attitude.

Meditating is natural, part of who you are. Keep it real simple. You are already meditating during your daily life, more often than you realize. So here's the trick: Just try to be a bit more aware of how you meditate during each day—that way you'll find more of the peace you looking for, have more fun, and enjoy a richer, fuller, more successful life in every way possible.

THE NEW MEDITATION

Do What You Love—the Meditation Will Follow!

Here are examples of the many activities millions of busy Americans already enjoy—each is a perfectly natural way to meditate

Running—30,000,000
Fishing—50,000,000
Hiking—72,000,000
Cycling—85,000,00
Tennis—25,000,000
Golf—25,000,000
Yoga—18,000,000
Tai Chi—10,000,0000
Martial Arts—6,000,000

******

TM practitioners—5,000,000
American Buddhists—3,000,000

INTRODUCTION

WHO TOLD YOU "SITTING" IS THE *ONLY* WAY TO MEDITATE?

Mention the word "meditation" and most people immediately think of *sitting* meditation. You probably get a mental image of Tibetan monks sitting silently in the lotus position. The media reinforces this popular image with articles and books that give us the impression that sitting meditation is the *only* way to meditate. This emphasis on sitting meditation is understandable, having evolved slowly over the past thirty years. Three trends created and reinforce this belief:

TREND #ONE
MEDICAL PROFESSION FOCUSING ON PASSIVE RELAXATION

Cardiologist Herbert Benson's 1975 bestseller *The Relaxation Response* described how mental stresses create physical diseases. Stress was inherently damaging, the solution was stress reduction. Based on his studies of Tibetan monks and Transcendental Meditation practitioners, Benson put into simple layman's language the steps for effective sitting meditation. Actually, Benson was merely redefining what the old masters have been doing for centuries.

Unfortunately, the sixties hippies were also 'into' Eastern mystics, making the public leery of their meditation. As a result, Benson's relaxation response proved to be a stroke of marketing genius, giving "meditation" a new legitimacy separate from the hippie drug culture, while paving the way for a wave of new stress reduction clinics that emphasized sitting meditation.

TREND #TWO

DALAI LAMA WINS THE NOBEL PRIZE AND HOLLYWOOD'S HEART

The Dalai Lama was awarded the Nobel Peace Prize in 1989. Since then Tibetan Buddhism has fascinated the American public, while taking over the media spotlight on a regular basis. In 1997 Hollywood released two films about the Dalai Lama: Scorsese's *Kundun* and Brad Pitt's *Seven Years in Tibet*.

Thanks to the public charisma and quiet charm of this humble man, the number of Buddhist meditation centers has increased dramatically in America. And as we search for new ways to cope with the increasing level of stress in Western culture, the Noble Peace Prize has triggered a steady stream of articles and books on Tibetan culture, the Buddhists' peaceful way of life and Eastern methods of sitting meditation.

TREND #THREE

BULKY MRI MACHINES LIMIT RESEARCH TO STATIONARY SUBJECTS

In the eighties, magnetic resonance imaging (MRI) became the primary diagnostic tool for neuroscientists, stress reduction clinicians, psychologists, physicians, and other mind/body researchers studying the meditating brain. The powerful MRI scanning technology helps professionals "see" and analyze human emotions and decision-making using colorful pictures of the brain, which also make great illustrations in media coverage on meditation.

Unfortunately, MRI machines have some major limitations: They're bulky and immobile, weighing tons and costing millions. As a result, neuroscientists and stress management experts limit themselves to testing stationary subjects, such as Tibetan monks, rather than athletes and other moving subjects. Hopefully in the future the neuroscientific community will recognize the inherently unscientific bias of research that ignores 80 percent of America's meditators.

INTRODUCTION

SITTING MEDITATION GETS MEDIA SPOTLIGHT

These three trends came together recently when the Dalai Lama and Tibetan Buddhist scholars from around the world participated with Western neuroscientists and stress management professionals in a widely-publicized "Investigating the Mind" conference at Massachusetts Institute of Technology.

Science magazine called the conference a significant merger of Eastern and Western cultures: "Buddhists, with their 2500-year history of introspective inquiry into the nature of the mind, have much to offer neuroscientists." However, one skeptical neuroscientist expressed concern about the obsession to "get the electrodes on the monks." In spite of that, the conference was successful and sitting meditation is still center stage.

These three trends also tell us why our meditation bookshelves are stocked almost exclusively with books on sitting meditation; and why articles on meditation in the popular press are invariably illustrated with MRI brain scans and photos of monks sitting passively in the lotus position.

OUTSIDE THE SPOTLIGHT
A HUGE GRASSROOTS REVOLUTION IS GROWING

While all these neuroscientists, doctors and stress management clinicians have been *limiting* the definition of meditation to sitting, an underground movement has been quietly moving in the opposite direction and *expanding* the definition of meditation. Most of these people discovered through trial and error that sitting meditations doesn't work well for them, so they've been searching for alternative ways to manage stress and enhance their lives.

DOLLARS & SENSE OF MEDITATING

MENTAL BENEFITS
increased focus, discipline, sharper competitive edge, work efficiency

PHYSICAL BENEFITS
greater energy, healthy immune system, coordination, peak performance

FINANCIAL BENEFITS
increased productivity, income and wealth, improve your bottom line

PSYCHOLOGICAL BENEFITS
stress reduction, concentration, improve relations, peace of mind

SPIRITUAL BENEFITS
awareness, compassion, ethical living, becoming a whole person

INTRODUCTION

THE FOUR MEDITATION ZONES
mental * sports-fitness * creativity * relationships

FOR OVER THIRTY years the public's image of meditation has been narrowed almost exclusively to sitting meditation. Meanwhile, a quiet grassroots revolution has been exploding outside the media spotlight. Meditation is being redefined by millions of normal people who have discovered that sitting meditation does not work for them. So they are deciding for themselves what kinds of meditation work best for them, and turning to alternative approaches, without the help of traditional meditation experts.

RADICAL NEW APPROACH
STRESS IS POSITIVE, HEALTHY & ENERGIZING

This shift is most obvious in comparing the *Relaxation Response* of Dr. Herbert Benson with the work of sports psychologists such as Dr. James Loehr and his *Challenge Response.* They approach stress from opposite directions.

Dr. Benson and the medical profession come from a belief system that focuses on disease and pathologies: Stress is bad. It damages the body. In contrast, sports psychologists see stress as challenging, yet positive and healthy. When Loehr says "everything you know about stress is wrong" he is challenging the underlying belief system of the medical profession.

For the past couple decades, sports psychologists have been proving that stress is healthy, that stress is positive and natural for humans, and that stress is not only manageable, it helps us tap into a powerful inner resource that is constantly challenging us to reach for our highest potentials, as athletes and as humans. In this new paradigm, stress is neither bad nor to be avoided, it is seen as a positive challenge and a powerful source of energy.

THE NEW MENTAL TOUGHNESS
THE DOORWAY TO MEDITATION-IN-ACTION

The "mental toughness" approach of Loehr and other sports psychologists use works along with developing physical toughness. The goal of mental toughness training is to *increase* your capacity to handle stress in work situations. Not by avoiding stress but by working with the stress challenges in ways that build inner strength and help you reach new levels of performance.

Sports psychologists realize that an approach focusing on stress reduction is not enough in the sports arena or in the business world. In their research, Loehr and his business partner Dr. Jack Groppel discovered that: "The performance demands that most people face in their everyday work environments dwarf those of any professional athletes we have trained."

The influence of these corporate/sports psychologists can be seen everywhere in the examples below in the Sports/Fitness Zone. Their approach—integrating the mental, physical, emotional and spiritual—has opened the door wide for other ways of meditating in the creativity and relationships zones.

A PASSION TO CREATE
THE ARTIST'S WAY OF LIFE AS MEDITATING

Another quiet counter-trend is having an equally powerful influence on the new ways people are meditating today, expressed in the reemergence of the creative spirit for average people rather than the arena of professional artists. Many works—such as Julia Cameron's *The Artist's Way,* Betty Edwards' *Drawing on the Right Side of the Brain,* Wayne Dyer's *Real Magic,* Thomas Moore's *Care of the Soul,* and others are an expression of this elusive spirit of creativity in America, as a way to meditation and a new kind of spirituality.

INTRODUCTION

TAKE THE 10-DAY CHALLENGE
DISCOVER WHAT REALLY WORKS FOR YOU

**Start Meditating Today!
Remember
Anything You Love Doing
Can Be Your Meditation
*Anything!***

HOW DO YOU know if you've got the right meditation for you? Well, first of all, you've come a long way knowing what doesn't work—just knowing that you're one of the four out of five Americans who've already tried sitting meditation and know it is not the best way for you. Still, you live in a high-pressure world, you've heard that meditation has benefits, and you're persistent.

So how can you find out what's right for you? Here's a little experiment: Start with the next ten days, then work out the details over the coming months. Start today and pick some of your favorite experiences in all four zones and *practice the four basic rules in each.*

You might, for example try some simple count-to-ten breathing, a walk at lunch, jogging, or listening to your favorite music while commuting to work. You decide the activity. Then focus and apply the basic rules. This is your experiment.

Then continue one day at a time, expanding your efforts for ten days. Go slow. On day two you might try it while writing in your journals, reading to your child, or on your next trip to the health club, meditate in sauna. Each day go back, read about a new way people meditate. Try different ones that fit your personally. Use the four rules.

xxi

DO WHAT YOU LOVE
THE MEDITATION WILL FOLLOW

Each day focus on some activity you already love doing. Stay totally in the moment while doing it—for a few seconds, minutes or maybe even for hours. Practice meditating whenever the mood hits you. Eventually you'll discover that your whole life is filled with opportunities to meditate—*that your life is a meditation.* However, for now, the next ten days, just focus and meditate consciously on activities that feel right without pushing it. And remember, there is no wrong way, only your way. Trust yourself, you will find it.

That's the test, that's how you know that what you're doing is the right way to meditate—it comes naturally and you love doing it! The focusing on the moment is easy. And whatever you pick to work on, you're passionate about it! Trust that knowing. You'll see how easy it is to lock on and focus on what you're doing because it makes you feel better about yourself and you enjoy doing it. Meditation is not medicine. If it's not right, you'll know, move on, try something else, make sure you feel good while trying this approach.

JOIN THE CLUB!
DISCOVER HOW TO GET RICH IN SPIRIT & IN FACT

Need help? If you're in your favorite bookstore or at home, find a comfortable chair, sit for a while and read a few chapters that sound familiar to you. See how millions of people find ways of meditating by trial and error: running, painting, gardening, walking, listening to music, playing golf, yoga, dance, fly-fishing, writing, tennis, reading, rockclimbing, sitting in a sauna, volunteering, the list goes on. Each has discovered a new way of meditating that works for them.

You have to find your own way. Fortunately, millions are already blazing a trail. Why? Because it's natural, instinctive and easy to do. You meditate by doing something you love, you focus, you do it with passion, you chose your own way of meditating. It's easier than you think. In fact, you're probably already doing it!

That's the program: Today, ten days, a month, a year, and then continue on, make it a lifetime of meditating, make meditation a way of life and live a healthier, happier, more successful life.

INTRODUCTION

The Dalai Lama's Smile
What's His Big Secret?

The great masters smile because they understand a big secret that few of us get—*meditation isn't difficult*. Meditation seems difficult because it's a mirror reflecting our lives. We make our lives difficult—and the masters see it reflected in our meditation.

But they won't tell you, you have to find out for yourself, you have to know it in your bones. So they play a game. They help you by making everything even more difficult than it is. They will set up obstacles, send you on wild goose chases, ask impossibly absurd questions, running your brain in circles.

Why this nonsense game, this wild goose chase, this elaborate hoax? Our lives are difficult enough and yet our minds keep making matters unnecessarily more difficult with our obsessive thinking. And to make matters worse, we're constantly looking for someone to tell us what to do, someone to blame when things go wrong.

The enlightened one, Gautama Siddhartha Buddha, actually figured that one out 2,500 years ago. He came up with one fundamentally simple rule: "Believe nothing, no matter where you read it or who has said it, not even if I have said it, unless it agrees with your own reason and your own common sense." Unfortunately, most people still don't get this simple truth today. We still want some guru, boss or authority to take responsibility, so we don't have to. That's human nature. That's why life is difficult.

The day came when Buddha decided it was time to pick his successor, someone who could pass on this new way of living. He came into the great lecture hall. Everyone sat patiently, expecting the great one to give them yet another lesson telling them how to live the good life, how to make their living less difficult.

But this time The Buddha said nothing. The crowd became restless, they wanted answers, the truth, instructions on what they should do next. Still silence. After sitting a while, Buddha silently held up a lotus flower. Everyone was baffled, except one savvy monk. He got it. He began smiling. Buddha winked back. He had his man.

The same happens today, a nod, a wave, a secret handshake—you get it, you're in. The master smiles when you smile, when you finally figure out that life isn't as difficult as your brain makes it. Meditation is a mirror on your life, and a doorway to living with a smile.

Make your meditation—and your life—less difficult, discover your smile!

THE TRADITIONAL **MENTAL ZONE of MEDITATION**
10 familiar ways for sitting meditations

1.1 — **THE RELAXATION RESPONSE**

1.2 — **BREATH COUNTING**

1.3 — **MIND/BODY SCANNING**

1.4 — **MANTRAS & CHANTING**

1.5 — **MINDFUL & COMPASSION**

1.6 — **POSITIVE AFFIRMATIONS**

1.7 — **CENTERING PRAYER**

1.8 — **INSPIRATIONAL READING**

1.9 — **THE OFFICE BREAK**

2.0 — **CAREER & LIFE PLANNING**

1.1 RELAXATION RESPONSE

THE RELAXATION RESPONSE
AS MEDITATION

> *The relaxation response can be elicited by*
> *a number of meditative techniques ... There are*
> *two basic and necessary steps which I found*
> *to be present in practices in every culture:*
> *the repetition of a sound, word, phrase or prayer; and*
> *the passive setting aside of intruding thoughts*
> *and returning to the repetition.*
> Dr. Herbert Benson,
> The Science of Meditation
> Psychology Today

DR. HERBERT BENSON is acknowledged as America's leading pioneer in the field of stress management. Three decades ago this no-nonsense medical doctor surveyed the impact of stress on physical health, emotional well-being and workplace productivity and concluded that we had an epidemic on our hands—with 60-90 percent of all doctor visits the result of stress-related conditions.

When he wrote *The Relaxation Response* back in the mid-seventies he was building on a couple decades of research at Harvard Mind/Body Medical Institute—he had surveyed stress problems, meditation and stress reduction techniques going back 4,600 years. He also noted that in recent times, although technology "was supposed to make life easier for people, it often seems to intensify the stress in our day-to-day existence." Fortunately, in meditation Benson discovered a proven, low-tech solution that effectively reduced stress.

THE MENTAL ZONE

NEW NAMETAG BRINGS ANCIENT TOOL MAINSTREAM

Back in the seventies, however, the word "meditation" conjured up too many images of new age gurus, spaced-out hippies, beat generation poets and Eastern swamis. But in a marketing tour de force Dr. Benson set aside the "meditation" nametag and repackaged "meditation" as the "relaxation response." And thanks in part to that brilliant move, the book sold millions of copies and made sitting meditation acceptable to mainstream Americans.

Secondly, Benson's "relaxation response" approach was also brilliant in the way he was able to summarize the essence of all sitting meditation practices into just two simple steps that anyone anywhere could easily grasp and follow—just two simple steps that he "found to be present in practices in every culture" throughout history and across the world.

In other words, the relaxation response was not some new gimmick, but a universal path that has a proven track-record going back thousands of years, embracing all continents, nations, religions and historical periods, which explains why it works at such a basic human level.

GO HIGH-TECH & "MEDITATE LIKE A ZEN MONK"

Benson's formula is deceptively simple to grasp. First, let's review the ultra-basic two-step short-form of his relaxation response. It consists of "the repetition of a sound, word, phrase or prayer; and the passive setting aside of intruding thoughts and returning to the repetition."

Now do you think the relaxation response is a bit too simple? In fact, most people can't believe anything so simple could possibly reduce *their* stress.

So what do people do in today's high-tech era to accelerate the process? They run out and buy meditation tapes based on ads that promise you'll be able to "meditate deeper than a Zen monk, literally at the touch of a button." Then they buy high-tech sound systems, DVD players, headphones, cushions, bells, incense, oriental rugs, and other props before they even begin meditating, believing that all

1.1 RELAXATION RESPONSE

the high-tech equipment and ritualistic props are what meditation is all about.

DOES TECHNOLOGY MAKE LIFE MORE PEACEFUL OR INCREASE STRESS?

Our modern minds are so steeped in quick fixes, sophisticated theories, vicarious experiences and the hottest new technologies that we find it hard to believe anything could be so simple—and that's the problem!

Our complex high-tech high-speed world is creating most of our stress problems, not making life easier and more peaceful. Some experts estimate that the daily *New York Times* has more information than a person would see in a lifetime back in medieval days before the invention of the Guttenberg press. No wonder we're overloaded, overwhelmed and over-stressed.

EVERYTHING YOU NEED TO KNOW FOR A SITTING MEDITATION

We need to simplify life and slow down. In short, we *need* tools that work like the relaxation response! The book has sold millions of copies, so we know Benson's doing something right. Here's the good doctor's simple prescription:

---

1. **Pick a focus word, phrase, or prayer rooted in your belief system.**
2. **Sit, get comfortable and close your eyes.**
3. **Relax your muscles. Start with feet, work slowly up to your head.**
4. **Breathe naturally and say your focus word as you exhale.**
5. **Keep a passive attitude. Don't worry about how well you're doing. And if any thoughts come to mind, simply say, "Oh well," and gently return to your repetition.**
6. **Keep doing it for ten to twenty minutes. When you're done, sit quietly for a minute, let your thoughts come back before opening your eyes, then sit for another minute before standing.**
7. **Practice this technique one or two times a day, whenever convenient.**

Some years later, after striking up a friendship with the Dalai Lama, Benson made several trips to India where his team studied the mediation practices of exiled Tibetan monks.

HARVARD DOCTOR GOES TO INDIA
IMPROVES ON RELAXATION RESPONSE

While in India, Benson's team "witnessed incredible mind/body feats" done by the monks, such as raising their body temperature sufficient to survive in freezing weather cloaked only in a loin cloth. After that he began teaching his patients a revised two-step meditation process to reproduce what the monks were able to achieve:

"First you evoke the Relaxation Response and reap its healthy rewards. Then, when your mind is quieter, when focusing has opened a door in your mind, visualize an outcome that is meaningful to you ... If you are concerned with your performance at work or on the golf course or tennis court, imagine yourself performing well in those venues. Whatever your goal, these two steps can be powerful, allowing yourself to reap the benefits of the Relaxation Response and take advantage of a quiet mind to rewire thoughts and actions in desired directions." In short, sitting may not be the best way to meditate.

Bottom line: The relaxation response is sitting meditation at its simplest and most effective, a perfect stress reduction tool. And for many, the benefits will be experienced almost immediately—without a lot of expensive props and high-tech equipment. Just do it and you will slow down, feel a sense of calm and peace of mind, and be able to work more effectively and productively.

BEYOND SITTING MEDITATION
A NEW WORLD OF PEAK EXPERIENCES

Try it. Experiment. You may want to start with sitting meditation. It may turn out to be the best one for you. And if this fits your personality, once you have a solid foundation in the relaxation response, take Benson's advanced action-oriented course on "the spirit of peak performance" in his latest book, *The Breakout Principle,* coauthored with William Proctor.

1.1 RELAXATION RESPONSE

Benson calls his new breakout principle the "ultimate self-help principle." In the new *Breakout Principle* he discusses the six major life-cycle "triggers" that help people go beyond the basic stress reduction benefits of meditation and the relaxation response, and into a new level of awareness—*a breakout*—which is also not a new concept but rather a description of a profound experience that has been described by spiritual masters in various ways throughout history—as an epiphany, higher consciousness, an awakening, enlightenment, satori, ah ha! and other familiar names.

Following successive breakout experiences, Benson says the meditator moves into a more energized life filled with *peak experiences—in productivity, health, athletics, self-awareness, creativity, altruism, and total transformation.* In reality, the breakout experience has been with us all along as a natural result of any regular practice of the relaxation response, and indeed the natural result of all meditation practices for thousands of years.

If you want more specific examples you'll find them below—*turn to our sections on the Sports-Fitness Zone, the Creativity Zone and the Relationship Zone*—for lots of examples of meditation methods that are already being used by the four-out-of-five Americans who have discovered that sitting meditation isn't the best kind of meditation for them.

THE MENTAL ZONE

BREATH COUNTING
IS MEDITATION

*This is a warning: Stress may kill.
Literally. (The bodily version thereof.)
And it surely kills effectiveness!
Antidote? That's up to you.
A few deep-breathing breaks, or
two-minute-eyes-closed meditative stints,
can be invaluable during the course of the day.
So, too, a long holiday—and
the occasionally four-day weekend.
Such breaks are essential ...
One more thing,
the tougher the circumstance,
when breaks are impossible,
the more you need a break.
Tom Peters*

WANT A SIMPLE way to regain your composure, balance and peace of mind during a tense day, maybe right in the middle of a rough meeting—*breathe!* Just ten seconds will do. Works for me. Don't make a big fuss about it, just breathe and notice what you're doing. And since everyone else in the meeting is breathing, the chances are nobody will pay any attention to you.

The key is that you're not just breathing automatically, you're taking control of your breathing, and paying attention to how you're breathing.

Of course, that's a problem causing stress for most people today—we all breathe, *but we're not really aware of our breathing!*

1.2 BREATH COUNTING

And under stress, our breathing slows, lessening our intake of oxygen, lowering our effectiveness while increasing the strain on our physiological and psychological system.

SUCCESS IS BEING AWARE JUST 10-SECONDS MORE TODAY THAN YESTERDAY

So do it right now, in the middle of any meeting—*takes just ten seconds*—one deep breath, five seconds on the intake, five on the outtake. And while you're at it, tell yourself something positive, be grateful. Then take another ten-second breather. And later another. Become aware of your breathing.

And if you want to get mildly dramatic—*and make a statement*—stand up, walk to a window, stretch your arms way out wide, and silently feel like you're in control of the meeting. Take a deep breath, slowly. Just ten seconds. Then *without comment,* sit down, your actions say it all and I'll bet you'll even get a positive mental attitude out of the experience.

"If today you can be aware of breathing for ten seconds more than you were yesterday," says Dr. Andrew Weil in *Breathing: The Master Key to Self Healing,* "you will have taken a measurable step toward expanded consciousness, deeper communication between mind and body, and integration of your physical, mental, and spiritual functions. I can recommend no single more powerful, or more simple, daily practice to further your health and well-being." Try it, what do you have to lose? What do you have to gain!

That's quite a powerful endorsement of a few extra ten-second breaths a day. Should be enough to get you down to your favorite bookstore. He's easy to find, you can't miss seeing the good-natured Doctor Weil with his bushy beard, shiny top, and a friendly "hi there, I hope you're feeling well" smile.

BREATHING CREATES OPTIMAL HEALTH IN EIGHT SHORT WEEKS

Doctor Weil is an American pioneer in integrative medicine. He'll help you put your breathing in context as you get healthy. How? By focusing on your whole person, nudging you into a healthy lifestyle of nutrition, physical fitness and meditation.

THE MENTAL ZONE

Grab the good doctor's best-seller, *8 Weeks to Optimal Health* next time you're in the bookstore. Then buy a cup of tea, sit quietly, relax and flip through the book, there's a message in it for you. Just remember, the good doctor's main point is very simple—just for today become aware of your breathing "for ten seconds more than you were yesterday." And you're on your way to optimal health.

You can increase your awareness by breathing in different ways: Count each breathe rather than timing them ... or exhale normally, then squeeze more out ... or breathe in the mouth, out the nose ... or breathe rapidly to stimulate, then slow breathing to relax ... or breathe in the left nostril, out the right. Remember, *just ten more seconds of awareness today than yesterday*—and you will increase your awareness of being alive, of breathing, being relaxed and fully occupying your mind and body.

MEDITATE USING A 24-SECOND GAME CLOCK COUNTDOWN

Here's an interesting breath counting meditation for athletes, accountants and others trapped in a world of numbers. You breathe over sixteen thousand times a day—most of the time unaware of this great breathing machine that keeps you alive. Well, here is one way to see if you're capable of taking full command of your body's breathing process, by seeing just how long you can count your breaths.

Dr. Wayne Dyer's "24-second clock method" of breath-counting may seem rather weird at first, but it's a great way to do a simple meditation technique that's probably the most time-honored meditation practiced throughout history in both Eastern and Western cultures. Here's how Dyer does his meditation while counting down the clock from a basketball game:

> Visualize a clock made of numerous lights outlining the number 24. Then I shift down '23.' My own personal rule at the beginning is to get the clock in my mind to go down from '24' to '0,' seeing each number light up. If at anytime in that interval I become distracted, or a thought pops into my mind for even a fleeting microsecond, I start the clock over at '24' and work it back to '0' without any intervening thought or mental distractions. This is the way of

1.2 BREATH COUNTING

learning to discipline yourself to concentrate on one thing and to empty your mind of all other thoughts. Getting all the way to '0' from '24' is a monumental accomplishment!

The game-clock version of the basic breath-counting meditation comes from Dr. Dyer's *Real Magic,* which is one of my favorite inspirational books and probably the greatest of all his books. You are strongly encouraged to read it while working this meditation for a period of time.

MEDITATION VS. THROWING AN ELEPHANT

Now if this method sounds too much like more work, stick with Weil's occasional ten-second deep-breathing, using it inconspicuously in your office ... and occasionally lengthen your time sitting in meditation by using the light-hearted approach suggested by popular *Fortune* columnist and CBS executive Stanley Bing in *Throwing the Elephant: Zen & The Art of Managing Up.*

"Meditation: Step One. Sit down. If you are already sitting, stay that way. Breathe. Breathe again. Breathing is good. Think about the alternative! Your goal is to reach a place where, no matter what happens in any given day, you just don't give a shit. This is more difficult than one might think. It is in the nature of human beings to care what happens to them. But this caring is a delusion and a relic of your pre-Zen existence. Remember—nothing matters. You could be the most powerful force in the universe and it still won't make a difference in the end."

Remember you're taking 16,000 breaths every day, try counting a few of them for ten more seconds today than you did yesterday—*you'll feel more alive just by being aware and conscious that you are the one doing the breathing.*

THE MENTAL ZONE

MIND/BODY SCANNING
AS MEDITATION

*Body scanning uses your inner awareness,
rather than your eyes, to examine your body ...
Body scanning is very much like looking in a mirror;
but the mirror is the awareness in your mind.
You can use this inner awareness to check whether
you have collected any unhealthy muscle tension ...
with time and practice,
scanning can easily become a habit as
automatic as looking in the mirror.*
Dr. Charlesworth & Dr. Nathan
*Stress Management:
A Comprehensive
Guide To Wellness*

IN TODAY'S FAST-PACED and demanding business environment most of us hate waiting, it wastes precious time and makes us anxious. But it happens all the time. A traffic jam. On hold for an important telephone call. Waiting for a deal to close. Client late for lunch. Airport lines. You name it. Waiting is stressful.

Mind/body scanning has a specific purpose—find out where in your body you're holding the tension, creating the stress, causing your pain. Where is it in your body? Shoulders? Neck? Forehead? Fists? Clinching your teeth? The problem is that for many executives, *the head and body don't communicate!*

When I was on Wall Street it took a few years of therapy to figure that out.

1.3 MIND/BODY SCANNING

RECONNECT THE BODY TO THE "TALKING HEAD"

Why the disconnect? Because most executives work in their heads—*thinking, analyzing, dealing, planning, negotiating, organizing, designing, scheduling.* We spend so much time in our heads, our heads get disconnected and isolated from our bodies and emotions, as well as the rest of our lives. It's as if we are two separate people.

In many ways the television news term, "talking heads," is an accurate description of so many business executives, not by choice but simply because we work in a fast-paced, high-tech world with its 24/7 demands for more and more performance.

This separation of mind and body creates stress. And scanning the body is a simple meditation technique that can help any executive improve the connection between brain and body—and ease the stress. And scans can take a little as a few seconds. For example, in *Stress Management, A Comprehensive Guide to Wellness*, Dr. Edward Charlesworth and Dr. Ronald Nathan describe a Type-A business executive who had a habit of clenching his jaw. His anxiety was so distracting he needed help from these stress management consultants.

CORPORATE AMERICA'S "CLINCHED JAW" EXECS NEED TO GET BACK IN TOUCH WITH THEIR BODIES

This uptight executive would clench his jaw all the time—whether he was running late for an appointment or headed off for a quiet family vacation. His habit was so bad it seriously affected him physically, emotionally and on the job. Their "Executive Scan" technique had the executive turn all of his annoying waiting periods from negative to positive experiences by using body scans to focus on the source of the stress.

After this executive got the hang of scanning, he began using stop signs and street lights as opportunities for scanning, turning the negative of waiting into a positive—*a few brief moments at a time*—and he even taped reminders to his speedometer.

The exercise was simple and effective. The goal is to become totally aware of and focused on the physical location of the stress in the body and *away from* the impatience, anger and stress that had been isolated in his mind. The simple process of *reconnecting* his brain with his body gave this executive the power to deal with his stress consciously—*both in the head and in the body, effect and cause.* Before long he was able to reduce the tension in the jaw and relax.

THE BASIC "BODY-SCAN MEDITATION" TECHNIQUE USED IN STRESS MANAGEMENT CLINIC

You'll find examples and scripts for body scanning in most of today's books on meditation, usually involving more time and a more relaxed environment than a few brief moments waiting for a street light to change. I've used them for years, you'll adapt your own style after you try a few. So try it for a while and see if they're right for you.

Here's one from Dr. Jon Kabat-Zinn, director of the Stress Reduction Clinic at the University of Massachusetts and another pioneer in the field of stress management. He says this "Body-Scan Meditation" is a "very powerful technique we use to reestablish contact with the body ... because of the thorough and minute focus on the body in body scanning, it is an effective technique for developing concentration and flexibility of attention simultaneously."

FOOT BONE CONNECTED TO THE LEG BONE ...

Here is Kabat-Zinn's prescription for one very simple body scan, from his classic, *Full Catastrophe Living: Using The Wisdom of Your Body and Mind to Face Stress, Pain, and Illness.* He suggests you start by lying on your back and slowly move your mind through the different regions of your body.

Of course if you're in your office and a bit self-conscious about lying down on the floor or a couch, you can just lean back in your chair and close your eyes. Or go for a walk at lunch and lie down on the grass in a local park. Whatever you do, relax and treat the whole exercise lightly—in fact, I strongly suggest you might even silently hum that lively ol' tune, Dry Bones! "The foot bone's connected to the leg bone, the leg bone's connected to the thigh bone..." and so on up the body. Here are the simple how-to steps:

"Start with the toes of the left foot and slowly move up the foot and leg, feeling the sensations as we go up and directing the breath

1.3 MIND/BODY SCANNING

in to and out of the different regions. From the pelvis, we go to the toes of the right foot and move up the right leg back to the pelvis. From there, we move up through the torso, through the low back and abdomen, the upper back and chest, and the shoulders.

"Then we go to the fingers of both hands and move up simultaneously in both arms, returning to the shoulders. Then we move through the neck and throat, and finally all the regions of the face, the back of the head, and the top of the head. We wind up breathing through an imaginary 'hole' in the very top of the head, as though we were a whale with a blowhole.

"We let our breathing move through the entire body from one end to the other, as if it were flowing through the top of the head and out through the toes, and then in through the toes and out through the top of the head."

RECONNECT HEAD WITH BODY—THEN "LET GO!"

Meditation books often describe body scanning as a "letting go." For example, Kabat-Zinn says, "by the time we have completed the body scan, it can feel as if the entire body has dropped away or become transparent, as if there is nothing but breath flowing freely across all the boundaries of the body." That is, by reestablishing contact between the talking head with the body, you naturally let go of the tension between the two—the lack of connection causes the stress.

Finally, "as we complete the body scan, we let ourselves dwell in silence and stillness, in an awareness that may have by this point gone beyond the body altogether." Then after a time you gradually start moving your body and slowly return to the everyday world, refreshed, with a sense of wholeness.

Meditation is about increasing your awareness—of the world within you and around you. A scanning meditation makes you aware of the incredible body you inhabit and what you're doing with it—where, when, how you're using it. And once you're aware, you can use that feedback to your advantage and do something to correct the situation, relax and enjoy some peace of mind.

THE MENTAL ZONE

MANTRAS & CHANTING
AS MEDITATION

*The word mantra means a word or phrase that has power ...
Mantra is a general name for formulas, verses,
or words that are believed to have
magical, religious, or spiritual significance.
Their purpose is to produce a change
in the mental state of the person who uses them ...
Mantras do not express a thought,
they generate a thought or even a
concrete manifestation of that thought ...
mantras have the purpose of
accomplishing an action.
Drs. Monaghan & Viereck
Meditation*

Back in the eighties I took a course in Transcendental Meditation (TM). They gave me my "secret" mantra in a private session with one of the Maharishi's meditation teachers. Today there are over 40,000 TM teachers worldwide. My teacher instructed me to share my secret mantra with no one. While my experience was short-lived, I'm convinced that TM is a powerful meditation tool *for the right personality types.* It's certainly one of the largest meditation programs in the world, with millions of followers.

In Dr. William Glasser's classic, *Positive Addictions,* published in the mid-seventies, Glasser referred to meditation as "the most popular of all the positive addictions" he studied. TM got a special endorsement: "Although many practices of meditation have proved

1.4 MANTRAS & CHANTING

valuable for centuries and still are, the general public was little aware of them until [the sixties] when the Maharishi Mahesh Yogi came on the scene."

MAHARISHI ALSO REPACKAGED ANCIENT TOOL FOR MASS MARKETING

Although Dr. Glasser recognizes that TM has numerous critics, still he's an admirer, much like Herbert Benson. Moreover, like Benson, the Maharishi took a practical system of meditating that "lay dormant for thousands of years," and made it readily available to the general public as a part of the daily lives. "One of the Maharishi's great contributions is his ability to remove much of the false mystery and most of the intellectual snobbery and religiosity from meditation … I would conclude that TM has grown because it has value."

That was the mid-seventies. Today they have expanded to include a Maharishi Corporate Development Program and the Maharishi University of Management, an accredited university offering bachelors, masters and doctoral degrees in business as well as the sciences, arts and humanities.

A POWERFUL WAY OF FOCUSING, STABILIZING & FREEING YOUR MIND

Mantras are quite different from affirmations. An affirmation focuses on secular and materialistic goals selected by an individual. Mantras on the other hand are time-honored words and phrases that have mystical and spiritual qualities believed to resonate with nature, with the universe and with the gods. When you practice the mantra, your being and soul vibrate with everything in your world, you are playing an instrument—*your unique instrument*—in harmony with the music of the orchestra universal.

In *Awaken the Buddha Within,* Lama Surya Das tells us that "mantra" literally means "something to lean the mind upon. And that's what a mantra can do. Mantra practice can be relied on as a quick, effective, and powerful way of focusing, stabilizing and freeing the mind" while creating a positive mental attitude.

THE MENTAL ZONE

Mantras are repeatedly chanted, sung or hummed, repeated aloud, whispered, or silently in the mind. You must find the way that best fits you. And you may end up using any and all the above methods in different circumstances and at various times of day—a different one, for example, for your meditations in the privacy of your home, another in church, others in public gatherings, and yet another in your office or at a business meeting.

In one sense you've been listening to mantras all your life, they surround us and often become part of us. You probably heard your first mantra sung by your mother when the words were irrelevant, a soft lullaby that totally relaxed and lulled you to sleep. Later it may have been monks chanting, gospel choirs, or popular music, even rap and hip-hop may have clicked as a mantra for you.

THE UNIVERSAL MANTRA "AH-OO-UU-MMM"

The oldest and best known mantra is the ancient sound 'a-o-u-m.' It comes from deep within your soul. You slowly follow your voice exhaling a long, deep breath while your lips and mouth move gradually from a loud wide-open "O" shape to a soft hum coming from deep in your throat through closed lips.

Practice it a few times: Close your eyes and try this mantra several times. Focus solely on the mantra as it changes pitch and intensity in your body, moving through a wide range of sounds, at first loudly as the lungs surge forth, then slowly and imperceptably as the lungs empty and the mouth naturally closes, notice how the manta moves gently through you into silence and back.

Slowly: "Aaah-oooo-uuuu-mmmm." Then sit with the silence for a short while. Then, when you're comfortable, take a slow, deep breath and do it again. Feel the power of the sounds vibrating throughout your entire body, the sensations as you and the mantra become one, resonating with the voices of the universe.

The national mantra for Tibetan Buddhists is "om mani padme hum," the Buddha is within. Hindus repeat the many names of Krishna. Yaweh from Hebrews. Allah for Muslims. Gregorian Latin chants for Christians. Many other spiritual words are used. In business, executives use mantras all the time, to reinforce goals, create confidence, enhance performance, instill discipline, and keep

1.4 MANTRAS & CHANTING

themselves in action, on track and focused on their goals, hoping their mantras are favorable heard by the gods.

BUT DOES REPEATING "OUM" OR "COCA-COLA" WORK?

If you become one of the millions who are successfully working the Maharishi's TM program you will at some point be confronted with some of the standard criticisms. My advice, listen with an open mind: However, while the criticisms may have validity, in the final analysis you alone have to discover what works for your unique personality type. In the end, you must make up your own mind. If TM works for you, the criticism is irrelevant. Here are two critiques written about the same time as Glasser's *Positive Addictions*.

In *Powers of Mind,* Wall Street commentator Adam Smith said the "great Indian sage Krishnamurti was scornful of the techniques of TM and the Prayer of the Heart. 'By repeating Amen or Om or Coca-Cola indefinitely you obviously have a certain experience because by repetition the mind becomes quiet ... this is the most stupid, ugly thing which any schoolboy can do because he's forced to ... ' His own meditation was nothing: a blank empty mind."

And in Lawrence LeShan's classic, *How To Meditate,* we are warned that "if a guru tells you that he is imparting 'secret' knowledge for special people (like you) and that you must swear never to reveal it to the uninitiated, I advise seeking the nearest exit immediately. Can you imagine a Socrates, a Jesus, a Buddha telling his disciples that his wisdom was to be kept secret?"

Just remember, in the final analysis you and you alone are the sole judge of whatever meditation practice is the best fit for you. Go with your personal experience, and ignore both the critics and the disciples. If you and your personality type are suited to mantras, you'll know it instinctively—just give it a fair shake first, then try something else.

THE MENTAL ZONE

MINDFULNESS & COMPASSION
AS MEDITATION

> *Mindfulness is an ancient Buddhist practice which has*
> *profound relevance for our present-day lives.*
> *This relevance has nothing to do*
> *with Buddhism per se*
> *or with becoming a Buddhist,*
> *but it has everything to do with waking up*
> *and living in harmony with oneself and the world.*
> *It has to do with examining who we are,*
> *with questioning our view of the world*
> *and our place in it, and cultivating some*
> *appreciation for the fullness of*
> *each moment we are alive.*
> Dr. Jon Kabat-Zinn,
> *Wherever You Go,*
> *There You Are*

Most people are sleepwalking through life. We operate on auto-pilot like machines, reacting mechanically to external events according to programs hard-wired in our brains telling us in advance what the world expects of us—from parents, spouses and children, bosses, employees, friends, preachers, politicians, advertisements, newmakers, and others "out there."

Most of our lives are controlled by this stimulous-response relationship between our computer-brain and "them." As a result we respond as expected rather predictably, without critical thinking about our assumptions, values and reality—we are sleepwalking.

1.5 MINDFULNESS & COMPASSION

LIVING MINDFULLY BETWEEN MEDITATIONS!

In truth, mindfulness is the one common goal shared by every meditation practice—and as such it is not so much a meditation technique as it is *a way of living.* In fact, mindful meditation is really only important as a lead-in to mindful living. And conversely, if you are already living in this state of mindfulness in your daily life, then obviously there is absolutely no need for any special sitting meditation techniques, because you're already living it.

Meditation is not a sport. Nor is it a game. Of course you could look at meditation as a pregame training—for the real game of life. Just remember, you're not competing to become the Tiger Woods of mindful meditators. *The goal is to be mindful between meditations, in daily living.* Mindful mediation does its job if it succeeds in waking people up from their sleepwalking state. If you're already living your life mindfully, then you're already winning the game and you really don't have to meditate, do you. Get it?!

THE SEVEN ESSENTIAL QUALITIES OF MINDFUL LIVING AND MINDFUL MEDITATIONS

In *Full Catastrophe Living: Using the Wisdom of Your Body and Mind to Face Stress, Pain, and Illness,* Dr. Jon Kabat-Zinn, director of the University of Massachusetts Stress Reduction Clinic describes the seven qualities of mindfulness living that work as a package. These are the attitudes that mindful meditation will help you develop so that they will gradually become part and parcel of your everyday life:

Non-judgmental. You must become an active witness of your experience instead of automatically labeling things based on preconceived ideas or wishful thinking. "The habit of characterizing and judging our experience locks us into mechanical reactions that we are not aware of and that often have no objective basis at all." This split is a cause of our stress. But unfortunately, this is a tough habit to stop because it is so mindlessly automatic, we don't even know we're doing it most the time. Mindful meditation becomes a training camp preparing us for the real game.

THE MENTAL ZONE

Patience. I know what you're thinking, this is a tough one in today's competitive business world. We want everything now! Patience is a tough one but necessary, a sign of wisdom that we're accepting life as it unfolds on its own timetable. Meditation can help us see how our minds waste a lot of time and energy creating unnecessary stress, worrying about the past or wishfully thinking about the future. Stay out of the past, and the future, stay focused only on what you're doing in the present moment.

Beginner's mind. Whether you are handling a difficult situation in business, with some investments, or in your family, "an open, beginner's mind allows us to be receptive to new possibilities and prevents us from getting stuck in the rut of our own expertise, which often thinks it knows more than it does." You also increase your chances of getting the answer right. In *Zen Mind, Beginner's Mind,* Suzuki says: "In the beginner's mind there are many possibilities, but in the expert's mind there are few."

Trust. One of the great lessons of mindful meditation is "developing a trust in yourself." On the other hand, sleepwalkers rely so much on external authorities and mental programming that they don't trust themselves. The great Buddha himself spoke to this issue: "Believe nothing, no matter where you read it or who has said it, *not even if I have said it,* unless it agrees with your own reason and your own common sense."

Non-striving. Yes, to succeed in the business world you need goals. And yes, you need to strive to achieve your goals every day and with your life goals. Unfortunately, we often become obsessed and consumed by our goals. They become our life—striving, achieving, accumulating, buying the latest gadgets and keeping up with neighbors. We are lost without balance. Meditation will help you see how you can succeed by flowing with the river some of the time rather than paddling upstream all the time.

Acceptance. Very few people accept reality. Instead, we "often waste a lot of energy denying and resisting what is already fact."

1.5 MINDFULNESS & COMPASSION

We want things different than they are, but this wishful thinking gets in the way of positive changes. Acceptance doesn't mean you have to like it, or have to resign yourself to fate and do nothing to change things. It simply means that you see things as they really are—*right now*—no matter what the facts are.

Letting go. At the heart of all Eastern meditation practices and their entire way of life is a concept of non-attachment, surrendering, detaching, letting go. Buddha's Four Noble Truths remind us that our lives are filled with frustrations, difficulties and suffering because of our attachments to ideas, beliefs, things, money, careers and people—but there is no permanence in an impermanent world.

Mindful meditation is designed to help you develop all seven of these qualities. But more importantly, *mindful living* means making these qualities part of your daily life, all day, every day—with close friends and loved ones, and with employees and bosses, customers and clients, the clerk in the store and the homeless guy on the street, and everyone else you deal with during the day.

If you are curious, take twenty minutes twice a day, sit quietly and simply witness your mind in action without judgment and without any attachments, and when any thoughts do come across your radar, gently let them go.

BEWARE OF GURUS WITH THE "STINK OF ZEN"

Many gurus in this arena tend to make mindful meditation far more complex and esoteric than it need be. For example, while I was a work scholar at the Big Sur's Esalen Institute we were given an opportunity to study Vipassana meditation from a known guru. I was very interested, Vipassana is the original meditation technique taught by the Buddha himself twenty-five hundred years ago.

Vipassana is also known as "insight meditation" because as it sharpens our sense of mindfulness, Vipassana brings us greater wisdom and insight into the nature of reality, and it is, therefore, considered a direct path to enlightenment.

About forty of us attended the session. The guru arrived and proceeded with his ten-minute warmup drill as he laid out all his props: An imported rug went down first, then fancy Indian pillows, a small carved mahogany table for sundry artifacts, little bells, incense holders, faux icons, a boom box with Hindu music, a skull cap, a cute shawl was draped over his shoulders to capture the true air of authentic guru spirituality, all while he spoke in a pretentious dialect, as if to let us know that he was more mindful than we were.

I walked out after a few minutes of the little drama—my gut told me he had nothing to teach, that he was caught up in what the ancient Zen masters called "the stink of Zen." But in retrospect, I now see *I was looking at my reflection in his mirror.* Someone with a true Zen spirit of the beginner's mind would have stayed, listened, looked deep into that mirror, and learned something. That's what mindfulness, insight meditation and vipassana therapy are all about, because *everyone is our teacher, everyone.*

SEARCHING FOR GURUS IN INDIA
FINDING THEM IN HOLLYWOOD, ON WALL STREET

Other masters, experts and authorities on Vipassana insight meditation will promote their classes, retreats, videos and audio tapes by emphasizing that Vipassana is a form of do-it-yourself psychotherapy. While it is true that Buddhist meditations have often been described as the East's alternative to Western psychotherapy, my experience has been that Eastern gurus and their Western disciples often become too dogmatic and rigid in their practices, with unhealthy results for several people in my life.

If you really want to learn about mindful meditation as a way to living a mindful life, forget about traveling to study with a guru on a mountain top in India or Japan, to get a mega-dose of mindful therapy—go to any Mind/Body and Stress Management Clinic right here in America, even in Hollywood. Alternatively, a sports psychologist or yoga instructor can save you time and money and very likely produce superior results.

1.6 POSITIVE AFFIRMATIONS

POSITIVE AFFIRMATIONS
AS MEDITATION

> *If you have a guy with all the survival training*
> *in the world who has a negative attitude and*
> *a guy who doesn't have a clue*
> *but has a positive attitude,*
> *I guarantee you that the guy with a*
> *positive attitude is coming out of*
> *the woods alive. Simple as that.*
> *Special Forces instructor*
> *in Fast Company*

AFFIRMATIONS ARE POWERFUL words and phrases that tap into our inner-most belief system and arouse your emotions. Unlike mantras—which are thought to be cloaked with spiritual and religious energy—affirmations have a more practical role in everyday life and are used every day in the business world. I have them everywhere, my desk, monitor, wallet, and on my mind, reminders when the going gets tough and the stress is high. You probably do too.

In fact, I believe all executives are familiar with and use affirmations in one way or another, although you may call them goals or mission statements, for example. Affirmations are natural expressions of what we want to achieve in business and in life, and the attitudes we need today to get what we want. My first contact with them came from Napoleon Hill's classic, *Think & Grow Rich*, which most of us in business have read at one time or another.

THE MENTAL ZONE

WHATEVER THE MIND CAN CONCEIVE AND BELIEVE, IT CAN ACHIEVE

You need a "definiteness of purpose:" Clearly state your goal, exactly what you want, when, your target date for achievement, a definite plan. Then you write it down, and read it aloud to yourself twice a day. Tape it to your bathroom mirror and put a copy on a card in your wallet—and read it often!

Hill's secret to getting rich is an affirmation he repeated "no fewer than a hundred times throughout this book" *to encourage you to create your own affirmations in writing!* Why? Because Hill believed with absolute conviction that, "whatever the mind can conceive and believe it can achieve," and over the years that belief has worked for millions in the business world.

There are many variations of his message—for example, Mark Fisher's wonderful little parable, *The Instant Millionaire;* Jack Canfield's wide-ranging *Success Principles;* and Wayne Dyer's *Real Magic*—but in the final analysis, Hill's classic is the benchmark against which all other motivational works are measured by the business community.

YES, YOU CAN "THINK & GROW RICH!"

Today there's one that does sail high over the bar. Moreover, it is the simplist and best description about how affirmations actually work to create success in today's highly competitive business world. It comes from Jack Canfield and Mark Hansen, the creators of the *Chicken Soup for the Soul* phenomenon.

In their tenth anniversary edition, *Living Your Dreams,* they tell us that "an affirmation is a statement that evokes not only a picture, but the experience of already having what you want." And as with *Think & Grow Rich,* you anchor the affirmation over and over: "Repeating an affirmation several times a day keeps you focused on your goal, strengthens your motivation, and programs your subconscious by sending an order to your subconscious crew to do whatever it takes to make that goal happen."

1.6 POSITIVE AFFIRMATIONS

THE CHICKEN SOUP FOR THE SOUL'S RECIPE FOR A PERFECT AFFIRMATION

Here's the simple *Chicken Soup* recipe for creating great affirmations that are guaranteed to work so that you can achieve all your goals in life. Just follow these eight simple rules in constructing your affirmations:

---

1. An affirmation starts with *"I am ..."*
2. An affirmation is always *stated in the positive.*
3. An affirmation is stated *in the present tense.*
4. An affirmation is *short.*
5. An affirmation is *specific.*
6. An affirmation includes an *action verb ending in –ing.*
7. An affirmation has a *feeling word in it*
8. Affirmations are *about yourself.*

And yes, affirmations do work, the two geniuses behind the *Chicken Soup* books are living proof of the incredible power of an affirmation.

Their first book received 121 rejections, and yet they never lost sight of their dream. Ten years later, they were closing in on 100 million in sales! So they upped the bar with a new affirmation—their "2020 Vision"—to sell one billion copies and raise $500 million for charity! Affirmations work. They are powerful success tools.

My personal experience with affirmations constantly amazes me in the way they seem to produce actual results. Maybe not always as fast as I wanted nor exactly as I had envisioned the results, but the results were usually blessings in disguise because what I actually did get was often much better than I could have hoped for.

And for that I am thankful because it proves to me that the process of using affirmations does work. It works because it gets you *into action with a positive mental attitude,* regardless of whether you end up where you planned to go or someplace even better.

ACCENTUATE THE POSITIVE, ELIMINATE THE NEGATIVE

So let me add one thing that you may need if you have any mental, emotional or spiritual resentments, because negative energy can subconsciously sabotage all the wonderful "Positive Mental Attitude" you're trying to create with your affirmations.

Always remember that the ol' Johnnie Mercer tune and make sure you're "eliminating the negative" as well as "accentuating the positive." Work out any resentments, anger, grief and what-have-you that might be holding you back and weakening your affirmations.

You need to balance the two, working on both at the same time, something I discovered through trial and error years ago during my midlife crisis. If necessary, work in private with your favorite therapist or spiritual counselor. The combination these two working together will create a powerful energy that's guaranteed to release the full thrust of your affirmations so that "whatever your mind can conceive, and whatever you believe, you will achieve!"

One final note on adding power to your affirmations—for the rest of your natural life, paste the words of the great Michelangelo on your bathroom mirror where you can see them every day: "The greatest danger for most of us is not that our aim is too high and we miss it, but that it is too low and we reach it."

CENTERING PRAYER
AS MEDITATION

*A young monk came up to
the great Zen master Dogen and
excitedly explained that
when he was deep in his meditation
the Buddha came to him surrounded
in a brilliant white light.
Dogen responded: 'That's nice.
Now just focus on your breathing
and it will go away.'
Zen wisdom*

DR. JOAN BORYSENKO is a psychotherapist and cell biologist. She is one of the leaders in the emerging science of psychoneuroimmunology—the study of how our thinking and behavior interact with our nervous and immune systems and ultimately affects our physical health. In *Fire in the Soul,* Borysenko says that "after many years of practicing different forms of meditation I settled into the practice of centering prayer, which I also like to teach because of its clarity, simplicity and effectiveness."

Put this in context: Remember that back in the seventies meditation of any kind, let alone a new field with an esoteric name like psychoneuroimmunology, was a radical departure from traditional medicine, which focuses primarily on sickness, physical diseases and pathologies, and relies primarily on drugs and surgery in healing the body's ailments.

THE MENTAL ZONE

SPIRITUAL OPTIMISM IN A SACRED WORD

Borysenko, along with Benson, Kabat-Zinn and others in the new field of stress management were shifting their focus from disease and sickness to wellness and health—to what she calls "spiritual optimism," wellness and a positive approach to life crises and problems, looking at them as opportunities for personal growth and a shift to the spiritual.

The great philosopher and theologian Pierre Teilhard de Chardin once described this shift in very simple terms: "We are not human beings having a spiritual experience, we are spiritual beings having a human experience."

Centering meditation is a perfect expression of this new spirit of optimism and positive thinking says Borysenko: It "involves the repetition of a sacred word chosen by the meditator, its focus is not on the sacred work per se, but on the inner silence. The word—which can be as simple as 'peace,' 'shalom,' 'Jesus,' 'let go,' or any other pleasing focus—is not repeated continually, but as a reminder to return to the silence when the mind begins to wander."

The practice of centering has deep roots in the ancient contemplative lives of Christian mystics such as St. John of the Cross and St. Teresa of Avila. Over the centuries contemplative living took many forms. In Ram Dass' *Journey of Awakening: A Meditator's Guidebook,* we learn that "reading scriptures, praying, and communing with nature were all forms of contemplation" by all mystics, East and West. Today we see how it has evolved in the Catholic mass.

SIMPLE GUIDELINES MAKE CENTERING WORK

Centering prayer was refined in the seventies by Fr. Thomas Keating, a Trappist monk. In fact, Borysenko says that Keating's book, *Open Mind, Open Heart: The Contemplative Dimension of the Gospel,* is "the single best book about meditation." In Keating's meditation the object of focus is the "divine presence." A set of simple guidelines for centering meditation were included in a recent *Spirituality & Health* magazine interview with Fr. Keating:

1.7 CENTERING PRAYER

"Choose a sacred word as a sign of your intention to consent to God's presence and action within. Choose a word during a brief prayer asking for the Holy Spirit to inspire you with one suitable for you, such as Lord, Abba, father, mother, amen, love, peace, or shalom..."

Sit in a comfortable position with eyes closed.
Settle into your silence.
Choose a sacred word as a sign of your consent
    to God's presence and action within.
Whenever you become aware of thoughts,
    gently return to the sacred word.
At the end of the prayer, remain silent
    with eyes closed for a few minutes.
Two periods of twenty minutes each day are recommended,
    one first thing in the morning
    and one in the afternoon or early evening.

That's it, the process of centering prayer and meditation is that simple. And I urge you to read Fr. Keating's book to learn more about how to make centering meditation a part of your everyday living.

TOUCH THE "DIVINE PRESENCE" WITHIN YOU—AND THE WHOLE WORLD

According to Borysenko this focus on the "divine presence" is what sets centering meditation apart from most other meditation methods—including body-centered meditations where "the focus phrase or mantra may be repeated either in rhythm with the breathing as suggested by Dr. Herbert Benson in *The Relaxation Response,* or without reference to breathing, as in transcendental meditation, as taught by the Maharishi Mahesh Yogi" and in the sitting meditation practices of Tibetan Buddhist monks.

Similarly, in *Open Mind, Open Heart,* Fr. Keating also distinguishes centering meditation by specifically mentioning that it is not a "relaxation exercise," nor self-hypnosis, nor a way to induce a high, nor a paranormal experience, and interestingly, he also says centering prayer is not a "mystical phenomenon."

When Keating adds that "even saints have misunderstood what God said to them," I was reminded of a wonderfully amusing little story often repeated for monks in training. A young monk came up to the great Zen master Dogen and excitedly explained that when he was deep in his meditation the Buddha came to him surrounded in a brilliant white light. Dogen smiled: "How nice. Now just focus on your breathing and it will go away."

A GENTLE DOWN-TO-EARTH SPIRITUALITY

Centering meditation has that same natural spirituality about it. Yes, the focus is on a word that expresses the divine presence in your life. Yes, you pick a sacred word rather than focusing on your breathing or repeating a mantra in an inconsequential language.

And yet, there is universal quality in Keating's emphasis, a quality that oddly (although he says otherwise) seems to drawn in and embrace the physical, mental and psychological aspects of life as part of this universal spirituality.

Indeed, as Keating puts it, centering meditation or contemplative prayer "is not so much the absence of thoughts as a detachment from them. It is the opening of the mind and heart, body and emotions—our whole being—to God, the Ultimate Mystery, beyond words, thoughts and emotions—beyond, in other words, the psychological content of the present moment. We do not deny or repress what is in our consciousness. We simply accept the fact of whatever is there and go beyond it, not by effort, but by letting go of whatever is there," a belief also engrained in centuries of Taoist and Buddhist thought.

INSPIRATIONAL READING
IS MEDITATION

*I never wanted to meditate.
I don't know why. I guess the
main reason is if I sit down to meditate,
I'm not getting my reading done.
That's been my main career—reading.
I remember Alan Watts once asked me,
'Joe, how do you meditate?' I said,
'I meditate by underlining sentences.'
I prefer the gradual path—the way of study.
My feeling is that mythic forms
reveal themselves gradually in
the course of your life.
Joseph Campbell*

YEARS AGO JOSEPH Campbell taught me this very simple message—*reading is meditation.* He meant the whole process of reading, studying, research, underlining, taking notes—*reading and meditation are the same thing.*

At another time Campbell made the same point when his friend Alan Watts asked him how he meditated. Watts was one of the great popularizers of Zen in America in the fifties and sixties, and a regular practitioner of za-zen, the Zen technique of sitting meditation.

Campbell saw meditation differently. Sitting meditation was a distraction from what he knew worked best for him. So he made his point with a light-hearted response, telling Watts that he meditated while "underlying," while doing his reading and his research.

THE MENTAL ZONE

READING IS A NATURAL WAY
THAT WE ALL USE TO MEDITATE

Reading inspirational literature, sacred texts, motivational and all kinds of other books is certainly the most commonly accepted form of meditation in the world. And today we would probably add listening to taped readings, although most so-called meditation tapes are boring. In particular, avoid any that promise you can "meditate deeper than a Zen monk at the touch of a button." Books have been proven meditation aids for thousands of years.

Books provide a natural way to meditate. The conventional wisdom in the press has most Americans believing that meditation can only be performed sitting in a lotus position with your eyes closed. And yet, we now know that any activity can be a meditation simply by applying the basic principles of meditation, staying in the moment, focusing on whatever you're doing—*including reading.* It's that simple. Reading is something we all do so naturally that we don't even think of it as meditation. And yet, it's the perfect mediation.

Reading has an incredibly long history as meditation, going back to the contemplative mystics of ancient times—Taoists reading the *Tao Te Ching,* Hebrews and *The Torah,* early Christians and *The Bible,* Zen masters and *The Ten Bulls* scriptures. The works of Aquinas, Meister Eckhart, and Goethe. And more recently, works such as Trappist monk Thomas Merton's *The Way of Chuang Tzu,* and *Zen and the Birds of Appetite,* and his friend, the Vietnamese Buddhist monk, Thich Nhat Hanh's *Living Buddha, Living Christ.*

THE "PEOPLE'S CHOICE AWARD"
HISTORY'S MOST POPULAR MEDITATION

Unquestionably, reading has been a favorite form of meditation for the great mystics of all times, all cultures and all spiritual traditions—reading is their way to enter and explore the eternal truths of the spiritual world as well as the tough questions about everyday human existence. In recent times, reading meditation has expanded far beyond monastic walls, offering unbelievable opportunities for everyone and anyone today!

1.8 INSPIRATIONAL READING

Everybody seems to be reading. Just walk into any Borders or Barnes & Noble. Everywhere from the children's section to the Starbucks lounge. The chairs are full, many of these people are reading and meditating. No mantras, no breath counting, no body scanning, and they don't call it meditation. It just is. They just do it to relax and reduce stress, to learn, to contemplate. Reading gets the 'People's Choice Award' for the most popular meditation in history!

YOU WILL BE GUIDED
TO THE RIGHT BOOKS FOR MEDITATION

Today anything you read can be an opportunity to meditate—*it is your decision!* Anything? Yes, whatever draws you to it. And you do not need to know why in advance. Trust you are guided. The obvious ones are in the spiritual, religious, inspirational, motivational and self-help shelves.

In addition, there's *Zen and the Art of Motorcycle Maintenance.* Others like *Zen & the Art of Knitting. Zen and the Art of Poker. The Tao of the Jump Shot. Golf for Enlightenment. Chi Running. The Tao of Surfing. Care of the Soul. A Course on Miracles. Zenvesting. Airplane Yoga. The Artist's Way. Money and the Meaning of Life. The Road Less Traveled. The Power of Now.* The list goes on and on. These are many of the obvious titles for reading meditation. They gently guide your mind along a natural path and into a peaceful world of contemplative meditation.

But who decides which books are the "appropriate" kind of reading for meditation? Or more particularly, who decides which ones are the "right" kind of books that will work for *your* unique style of meditating? Should you rely on the word of some external authority to decide for you? Can you trust a religious cleric, spiritual guru, university teacher, motivational coach or a hot-shot *New York Times* book reviewer to tell you which books are right or wrong for your meditations?

THE MENTAL ZONE

KANT, KING, COSMOS, CROSSWORDS & COMICS!

And how about novels? Maybe classics like *War and Peace, The Great Gatsby,* or Graham Green's *The Power & The Glory,* which gave me a new appreciation of Christianity. *The DaVinci Code* forced us to explore religious history. Grisham's *The Jury* makes you focus on the morality of our justice system. *Harry Potter* got huge numbers of young people reading. How about a Stephen King novel? Spy thrillers? Mysteries? Pulp fiction? Romance novels?

How about a book on Impressionist Art, Civil War military strategies, archeology, or 16th century mathematics? Browsing through home decoration books is one of my wife's favorite meditations. What about Carl Sagan's *Cosmos,* D-K's illustrated *Travel Guide to Italy,* or a Betty Crocker cookbook? Great food for your next meditation. Comics? They were my son's passion as a kid, they got him thinking about his career in the arts.

BERLITZ, BERRA, BIOTECH & BUSINESSWEEK!

But don't stop there. What about Berlitz language manuals, the *World Almanac,* books on repairing antique dolls, ballroom dancing, Yogi Berra's humor, medicine, nuclear physics, biology, legal ethics, even the boring tax code? Magazines? Why not? *National Geographic,* the *Smithsonian* and *BusinessWeek?* Of course you can meditate with them!

Yes, and even the telephone book can be a meditation aid. Years ago in a spiritual workshop the leader had a group of us pose a tough question. Then we randomly opened a telephone book, closed our eyes and randomly pointed to a word on that page. Next we had to trust that randomly selected word contained the key to the answer to the question, a message from the universal intelligence. Actually this presumably random process is quite similar to time-honored divination tools such as the Tarot, Runes and the I Ching.

YES, YOU DO KNOW WHAT'S RIGHT FOR YOU

The truth is, nobody can tell you what kinds of books are right for your reading meditation. No one. You and you alone know what works for you. And nobody else can ever tell you.

1.8 INSPIRATIONAL READING

Trust yourself. You will be naturally led to the kind of reading that is right for you. All you have to do is focus on what you are reading, set aside the distractions of the world and read—you are meditating. In Starbucks or Borders, in your local library, a park bench during lunch, curled up in bed late at night, on the commuter train to work, or right there sitting in your office—stop and read and meditate.

MEDITATION IS NOT A BOOK YOU ARE THE MEDITATION

By now you know that neither the kind of book nor the specific book you're reading is important—you are. This is the key point here, so let me repeat it again for emphasis: *The particular book you use for your meditation has nothing to do with whether you are meditating or not*—every book is an opportunity to meditate.

You have the absolute power to transform every book into a meditation. You alone can meditate on any book. *You are the meditation, not the book.*

When you understand that the meditation is within you—*that you are tapping into a secret power that is both within you and at the same time universal*—then you and the meditation are one and you know that whatever you're reading is just another tool to help you meditate. As Science of Mind founder Rev. Ernest Holmes tells us in *This Thing Called You:* "The answer is not in any book but in yourself." So trust yourself, you are being guided.

THE OFFICE BREAK
AS MEDITATION

> *The process of meditation is
> nothing more than quietly going within and
> discovering that higher component of yourself. ...
> It teaches you to be peaceful, to remove stress,
> to receive answers where confusion previously reigned,
> to slow yourself down, and ultimately,
> when you adopt meditation as a way of life,
> to be able to go into that peaceful place anytime.
> I do mean anytime.
> In the middle of a business meeting,
> in the midst of a tragedy, during an
> athletic competition—anytime.*
> Dr. Wayne W. Dyer
> Real Magic

OFFICE BREAKS ARE not only a perfect time to meditate, they are absolutely essential. Seriously, you spend eight hours every day, sometimes twelve or more hours, on the job, at work, confined to your office. All too often you're forced to complete one impossible task after another on an insane timetable. And yet, as every one us knows, our days are filled with big and little opportunities to meditate and reduce the stress. Take them, often!

CORPORATE ATHLETES NEED "TIME OUTS"

Office breaks fit into a cycle: "The key is to structure episodes of stress and recovery," says psychologist Jim Loehr, whose Corporate

1.9 THE OFFICE BREAK

Athlete programs are designed to help executives achieve peak performance at work. "You perform in waves. You cannot be at your best all the time, so you pick your times. And you have to pick your times of recovery as carefully as you pick your peak times ... You find ways to break the cycles of stress."

How? Take a tip from athletes. Loehr uses tennis players as an example. They recover fast, "between points. If they use that precious 25 seconds they're less likely to stress out." It's no different in the work environment, when 25 seconds may be all the time you have to meditate and recover from the latest cycle of stress—*you jump on the opportunity.*

BREAK THE CYCLES OF STRESS

There are so many simple ways to meditate during the work day. Many you already do naturally. A brief moment glancing at a family portrait, wishing success for one of your kids, health to a parent, hugs to your spouse. Maybe you could fill your office with some classical music. You could get a cup of hot water for tea and just sit feeling the warm cup. Just "sitting quietly, doing nothing," imagining you're at a simple Japanese tea ceremony, or relaxing at your favorite coffeeshop in the "Starbucks experience."

Or maybe just turn your chair around toward the window for a minute or so, lean back, close your eyes and repeat your favorite affirmation as a reminder of why you're doing what you're doing today and the goals that drive you. Take a moment and write a gratitude list, a short, quick list of all the special gifts you're grateful for this lifetime.

MAKE YOUR WORK A MEDITATION

The truth is, work often is a stressful grind, even when you're doing what you love. It feels like something you're forced to do out of duty, or just for the money, when you'd rather be doing something else. Even then your work can be meditation—out of necessity, to recover from the stress cycle. Yes, it's great to "do what you love and money will follow," but as paradoxical as it seems, a lot of the time you probably won't be madly in love doing what you love to do!

THE MENTAL ZONE

Remember, meditation is focusing in the moment on whatever you are doing—*living your life mindful and aware of what you're doing in this present moment, however it feels, good, bad or indifferent, there's no escaping the realities of your life.* So, in work and in meditation you focus only on what you are doing—*whatever it is, however it feels*—and nothing else. Period.

WHEN YOU WORK, FORGET THE COSMOS JUST FOCUS ON THE WORK

The first time I fully understood what this meant I was working with CBS MarketWatch. It was a very long day of hammering out columns and proposals, editing copy and tweaking the website. Finally I realized that it was dark out and very late. The day had passed while I was absorbed in my work.

Everyone else left a couple hours earlier. When I finished what I was doing, I packed my briefcase, shut off the lights, locked the doors and walked down the hallway to the elevators, alone. The long winding corridor walls had no artwork and were a dull, lifeless gray. Then out of the blue, I realized that I hadn't thought about God and the ultimate mysteries of the universe all day, which I occasionally do. Moreover, I hadn't *consciously* done any meditations during the day—*I became the work and was totally lost in it all day long.*

MEDITATING? ENLIGHTENED? NO BIG DEAL!

And as I walked down the hall I felt an overwhelming sense of peace with myself. Then I became amused with the fact that I hadn't thought about God all day, and yet, it occurred to me that maybe God, whoever he, she or it was, must of been thinking about me all day, while I was working. And that was okay.

Which reminded me of Veronique Vienne's delightful book, *The Art of Imperfection*. Toward the end she lists "ten good reasons to be an ordinary person," and the last fits here: "You are enlightened, though you don't know what it means, let alone care about it." That's the ultimate in meditation and in enlightenment. No big deals. Tomorrow you just get up and go to work again.

1.9   THE OFFICE BREAK

AN ATTITUDE OF GRATITUDE
THE ONLY MEDITATION YOU'LL EVER NEED

Perhaps even more important, I became profoundly aware that I had felt that same way many times before, I just didn't understand it was *peace* I was feeling, and I didn't have to label it anything. Moreover, it has happened often since then, for which I'm thankful.

Gratitude, the ultimate prayer. The great 14th century Christian mystic, Meister Eckhart once said "if the only prayer you say in your whole life is 'thank you,' that will be enough." Actually I learned that quickie meditation from a senior partner at Morgan Stanley that I worked with for many years. He said "thank you" often, even the smallest things. That impressed me. It's a habit what's stuck with me.

MEDITATING DURING BUSINESS MEETINGS

When I was with Morgan Stanley our offices were in the upper floors of the Exxon building in New York City. Investment banking is a demanding business, and intense work focusing on corporate financial, economic and legal documents. I needed frequent short meditation breaks throughout the day.

During staff meetings in the board room I'd sit with a view of the Hudson River and focus on airplanes coming in low on their approach. Often it was a toss-up between staying totally focused on the moment during one of those boring rah-rah meetings or concentrating on the moving aircraft. The slow flight paths of those planes often won, as a more satisfying meditation, better than counting my breaths or muttering a mantra in silence.

HOLLYWOOD MEDITATION
SERENITY PRAYER SPEEDS BORING NEGOTIATION

Later, after relocating to the West Coast, a Hollywood film producer client told me about how he meditated during boring and/or tense business meetings. He would mentally leave the meeting for a minute or so and say the Serenity Prayer or some other prayer.

He said it helped him put the meeting in perspective. That's right, those brief moments in meditation helped him better focus on the meeting when he returned mentally. When he was fully in the meeting he'd laser in on what he wanted out of the deal, without compromising. If he got it, fine. If not, the meeting was over, short and sweet, and he'd move on to something more important or more interesting that he really wanted to do.

GET ON YOUR KNEES & PRAY IN THE EXECUTIVE BATHROOM

If you're under stress, a few minutes in the restroom can be a great way of meditating, and holding onto your sanity! My first day with the Financial News Network I reported early, before we went on-air live. That very morning the *Los Angeles Times* published an expose detailing past financial shenanigans of the founder and president—the guy who hired me away from a successful position as associate editor of the *Los Angeles Herald Examiner!*

I was in the dark about the drama until I walked into the FNN studios my first broadcast day, about 5 a.m. and was barraged with questions from on-air talent and crew. After an embarrassing display of ignorance I ducked into the executive restroom, locked the door, got on my knees and said a brief prayer: "Okay whoever you are up there, you sure have an odd sense of humor. I hope you know what you're doing, because I don't." A brief meditation, then back into the action. Ten days later, the board terminated the president and I became the network's executive vice president and executive in charge of production.

In *The Corporate Athlete* psychologist Jack Groppel discusses a similar situation with an executive getting negative news just before walking into a major negotiation. A few moments in the restroom "recovering" from disturbing news was a good idea. Another would be a short five-minute walk, preferably up and down a few flights of stairs, "literally changing your heart rate and chemistry." Deal with the bad news before going forward.

CORPORATE ATHLETES TAKE CHARGE DO IT QUIETLY AND WIN

While each of us has our own individual path through life, most of us have one thing in common, work, and that means the office, with

1.9 THE OFFICE BREAK

all its stresses. To succeed as corporate athletes, says Groppel, we need to control our unique cycles of stress and recovery. And for all the differences, one of the surest ways to take responsibility is to approach your work day as a meditation, all day, every day—just don't take yourself too seriously, it's no big deal.

You don't have to think that what you're doing is spiritual. And you don't have to label what you're doing as meditation. When you take a break in the office—*that cup of tea or coffee, a warm glance at the family photo, a confidence-boosting affirmation before a big meeting, a quick thank-you for the gift of serenity during a tough negotiation*—you do not have to think "now I am meditating." You just do it, without making a big deal out of it. Remember, anything can be a meditation if you focus on whatever you're doing and nothing else—*"meditation" labels are not necessary!*

MEDITATION & ENLIGHTENMENT LIKE WINNING THE $50 LOTTERY

Live that way at work and you may get rich and maybe even get enlightened in the delightful way Veronique Vienne describes it in *The Art of Doing Nothing:*

"Reaching enlightenment is a bit like winning the lottery—not a million-dollar bonanza, mind you, just fifty bucks ... You probably weren't meditating. Chances are you were waiting for the light to change at an intersection, or looking out the window while talking on the phone ... On a scale of one to ten, it was probably a number four insight .... Enlightenment is just another word for feeling comfortable with being a completely ordinary person."

CAREER & LIFE PLANNING
AS MEDITATION

*As most millionaires report,
stress is a direct result of devoting a lot of
effort to a task that's not in line with one's abilities.
It's more difficult, more demanding mentally and physically,
to work at a vocation that's unsuitable to your aptitude ...
Millionaires who have a high creative intelligence often
make one very important career decision correctly:
They select a vocation that provides them with
enormous profits, and very often
this same vocation is the one they love.
Remember, if you love what you are doing,
your productivity will be high and your specific
form of creative genius will emerge.*
Thomas Stanley
The Millionaire Mind

WE'VE HEARD THE warnings a thousand times if we've hear them once: Stress kills! Seventy percent of all doctors' visits are stress related. Stress is costing business a couple hundred billion a year. High blood pressure. Heart attacks. Warning: Stress kills! Change now!

But few listen. We rationalize: That's the price of success. It's a jungle out there, with enormous pressures to perform, to succeed, hit a home run, bills to pay ... we're trapped, we make compromises, we tough it out, not me.

2.0 CAREER & LIFE PLANNING

MID-CAREER CRISIS—A VERY LONG MEDITATION

Then one day—*after years of pushing ourselves too much, watching the stress build, trying to hold everything together, at home, in the office, in our gut*—we finally go over the edge. Could be a health problem, emotional and family problems, job performance, maybe a spiritual crisis where you lose faith in yourself and all the values you were taught to believe.

Finally, you just can't take it any more, something pushes you over the edge. Whatever it is, big or small, something happens and you know you can't go on living the way your living. At this point nothing's working anymore—all the meditations and medications, prayers and affirmations, the therapy, trips to doctors, clerics and psychics, and the extra hours in the office—nothing.

You're running on empty. Everything you're doing to keep yourself in the game is gone, the passion you once felt for your career, gone, your edge, gone, you feel lost. Nothing's working. You even start reading books about burnout, the midlife crisis and the dark night of the soul.

THE TURNING POINT—SURRENDER TO WIN

Welcome, now you really belong in the club. We all go through these life-cycle and career turning points, sometimes more than once. And we all come out the other end successfully, even though it may take several years, so there are no quick fixes.

Reaching this point is actually a gift, because if you get to this point of acceptance, surrender and understanding—*where your way of doing things no longer works*—then you are open to change. You probably don't know what to do next, but you suddenly realize it can't be what you've been doing in the past. That's why this midlife dark night of the soul can be the greatest period of meditation and adventure in your life.

Fortunately, we eventually do come through the challenges with a renewed spirit, charging ahead in our careers—or moving into new and more exciting careers with a new sense of energy and passion. Two turning-point scenarios—and either way you come out a winner.

SCENARIO #ONE:
THE CORPORATE ATHLETE IN TRANSITION

The Corporate Athlete is a great example of the first of these turning-point strategies. These guys take a very positive approach. Instead of trying to reduce stress, they accept stress as a fact of life and focus on making stress work for you—*by increasing your capacity to manage stress.*

The program was developed by James Loehr, a noted sports psychologist and author of *The Mental Game* and *Toughness Training for Athletes,* and his partner Dr. Jack Groppel, author of *The Corporate Athlete.* And their unique, positive approach has a strong following. Regular clients come from Merrill Lynch, BMW, Dell, IBM, Disney, Ford, AT&T, Motorola and Travelers, as well as the FBI and ER physicians.

In fact, The Corporate Athlete program is so effective graduates of its three-day trainings—*which Fortune called both a "bootcamp" and "soul training"*—say it not only changed the way they work and improved their performance, it changed their entire lives. The Corporate Athlete program increases an executive's ability to handle stress in all areas of their life "not just a sharp intellect but also physical strength, emotional intelligence and a strong sense of purpose," plus strengthen their spiritual capacity, "the energy unleashed by tapping into one's deepest values."

HARDWIRING VALUES PLUS
A NEW SENSE OF PURPOSE IN YOUR SOUL

They refocus the way executives deal with everything from nutrition and fitness, rebuild a sense of purpose and confidence, and also introduce them to yoga and meditation. Ultimately, however, Loehr says "change only happens when it's powered by your values," and you "get it hard-wired into your soul."

One of the highlights of this bootcamp is a homework assignment requiring executives to answer five value-oriented questions that echo the core existential questions asked by contemplative mystics throughout history and in all traditions, Christianity, Judiasm,

Hinduism and Buddhism, questions guaranteed to revive your sense of purpose and values:

1. If you were on your deathbed and wanted to tell your children the three most important things you've learned in life, what would they be?
2. What gives you the greatest joy, satisfaction, and renewal in your life—and how could you do more of it?!
3. Who are you without your job and your money? Describe in detail.
4. What activities could you add to your life that would be a source of richness and joy?
5. Think of someone you admire deeply—and explain why.

The questions are designed to help you identify your core values, reconnect with them and start living them, with family and friends as well as in work.

And it works. In fact, one Wall Street director of sales operations says The Corporate Athlete program has changed hundreds of people's lives at the firm, helping "traders find more balance in their high-pressured lives." In short, the program is a perfect way to reenergize and refocus an executive going through a midlife crisis—assuming they're already in the career best suited for their personality type, as Stanley says in *The Millionaire Mind.*

SCENARIO #TWO
DO WHAT YOU LOVE—THE PASSION WILL FOLLOW

But what if you're in the wrong career? Well, if it's really wrong for you, then no amount of training to go back into the same old business again is going to help you—you *just don't belong there.*

I went through my midlife journey before The Corporate Athlete program was launched. For three years I struggled with staying on Wall Street with Morgan Stanley. I was doing a great job. In fact, *they* loved my work. But I wasn't a happy camper, in spite of all the money I was making. The money just makes a major career change more difficult as you compromise your values.

At night and on weekends during those years I saw a psychiatrist, wrote screenplays, took acting lessons, belonged to a dance meditation group and made short films at a Television Academy workshop. I even went to an astrologer after I heard J.P. Morgan regularly used them. By day I continued working on mega-million dollar investment banking deals with Morgan Stanley, but that no longer fed my soul.

Eventually I realized that I wouldn't be happy until I got into the creative arts business, somehow. So I quit and went to Hollywood. Life in the entertainment business was exciting for a few years. Then I got a doctorate in psychology—*yet another unexpected twist*—and worked as a career counselor advising business men and women.

And finally—at age fifty-seven, after years of searching—I realized that writing was the perfect outlet for my creative soul. I started working as a journalist, published a financial newsletter, and wrote several investment and personal finance books, plus *The Millionaire Code,* a career planning book that builds on the psychological profiling system first developed by Dr. Carl Jung.

CAREER & LIFE PLANNING
THE LONGEST MEDITATION & MOST REWARDING

Planning and replanning your career and your life-style is probably the single most important meditation you'll ever do in your lifetime. Very few executives ever make the break and get out of their career rut, so evident in Thomas Stanley's rhetorical question: "Why is it that only a minority of our population love their work?"

Career and life-style planning often begins when we get to that midlife cycle, start questioning why we're pushing ourselves so hard at something that's making us unhappy, stressed out and close to going over the edge. Planning, or re-planning your life and your career isn't just another meditation, it's the ultimate meditation, and sitting meditation isn't enough.

Yes, a comprehensive strategy like The Corporate Athlete is a great starting point. You may well be in the right career, just in need of a major retooling. I recommend trying something like that to begin the process. But if you're in the wrong career, you'll have to go on searching to find out why and what's next, in a larger living meditation that will go on for years.

HOW TO PICK THE RIGHT CAREER? PETER DRUCKER'S ULTIMATE TEST—VALUES!

In the final analysis, there is no right way, only your way. So while you're searching, here's how management guru Peter Drucker made his decision: "Many years ago, I too had to decide between my values and what I was doing successfully. I was doing very well as a young investment banker in London in the mid-1930s, and the work clearly fit my strengths. Yet I did not see myself making a contribution as an asset manager. People, I realized, were what I valued, and I saw no point in being the richest man in the cemetery. I had no money and no job prospects. Despite the continuing Depression, I quit – and it was the right thing to do. Values, in other words, are and should be the ultimate test."

What values most to you? Meditate, write about them, discover them, hardwire them deep in your soul. Become a true corporate athlete—*your way.*

THE SPORTS/FITNESS ZONE
10 ways to meditate & stay physically fit too

2.1—**RUNNING**

2.2—**YOGA**

2.3—**TENNIS**

2.4—**GOLF**

2.5—**WALKING & HIKING**

2.6—**MARTIAL ARTS**

2.7—**TAI CHI**

2.8—**SWIMMING & SURFING**

2.9—**FLY FISHING**

3.0—**GARDENING & DAILY LIVING**

THE SPORTS/FITNESS ZONE
OF MEDITATION

*According to an old Taoist saying,
'meditation in action is a hundred times,
no, a thousand times, no, a million times greater
than meditation in stillness' ...
There are indeed many activities that easily
lend themselves to meditation in action:
walking, dressing, bathing,
doing any repetitive task.
And finally, every aspect of living might
well benefit from the simplest and most
profound practices known on this planet.
George Leonard
The Way of Aikido*

THE CONTRAST BETWEEN Herbert Benson's "relaxation response" and Jim Loehr's "challenge response" offers us critical insight into why action-oriented meditations work better for most people rather than passive sitting meditation.

Like many in the business world, I thought there was something wrong because I just could not do any sitting meditation. Seems I tried all of them for years, they just didn't work for me.

Gradually, I realized that sitting doesn't work for most people. In fact, 80% of all Americans can't do it. I was normal! Sitting is just not the best way of meditating for most personality types as I discovered in working on *The Millionaire Code,* my book on how different personality types approach life in general, wealth-building specifically ... and meditation.

TO REDUCE STRESS, GET INTO ACTION!

The business world owes a lot to Dr. Herbert Benson. *The Relaxation Response* reintroduced America to meditation as it had been practiced for centuries in other cultures, from Buddhism 2,500 years ago to today's contemporary Transcendental Meditation. Benson helped us see the power of meditation in reducing the negative effects of stress on our bodies and minds.

In everyday language Benson told us how sitting meditation works, gave us a layman's scientific basis, and most important, he put meditation in a new, acceptable package—the "relaxation response"—which separated meditation from any negative associations with the hippy counter-culture of his day and popularized meditation with the general public.

MENTAL TOUGHNESS
THE CHALLENGE OF PEAK PERFORMANCE

Dr. Loehr, on the other hand, is a sports psychologist and author of *The New Mental Toughness Training for Sports* and *The Mental Game: Winning at Pressure Tennis* and *Stress for Success.* Like all sport psychologists, physical fitness trainers, team coaches and other professionals working with athletes, Loehr's clients are high-energy, action-oriented individuals who naturally respond to more active methods of meditation, rather than Benson's sitting meditations, which rely more on mental skills. Loehr's description of the challenge response is in marked contrast to Benson's approach:

"The final stage of mental toughness is reflected in the challenge response. You actually find yourself investing more positive intensity, more of yourself as the situation gets tougher. You find that problems you face in competition are not threatening but stimulating. You've gone well beyond simply loving to win. You have clearly come to love the battle. As a result of this emotional response, you have become an excellent problem solver. When everyone else is heading for the trenches as the problems start mounting, you smile inside because you know you got the emotional edge."

THE TWO-PHASE CYCLE
FIRST STRESS, THEN RECOVERY

The contrast between these two approaches is enormous. Benson comes from the perspective of traditional medicine, relying on the past, integrating age-old meditation tools. Loehr and other sports psychologists start with a fresh perspective built on modern science, looking to the future.

In addition, Benson focuses on creating the mind-body response of *relaxation*—slowing down, letting go, calm and peace. Loehr is at the opposite end of the spectrum, he focuses on the opposite mind-body response of *challenge*—intensity, stimulation, toughness and competition.

Both of them are dealing with the same well-known human cycle: Action, stress and performance followed by relaxation, rest and recovery. One natural cycle, two phases. As a result, Benson's emphasis on the relaxation phase of the cycle results in a preference for sitting meditation and mental processes. His goal is to condition the mind to better function in the real world when it returns to the action phase, but the emphasis is clearly on the relaxation phase.

Loehr's emphasis, on the other hand, is on the challenge phase of this natural cycle with a strong preference for action-oriented moving meditations that are better suited for athletes. Similarly, Loehr deals with the relaxation phase as part of the total natural cycle of action and relaxation.

STRESS IS A SOURCE OF POSITIVE ENERGY

Perhaps the most important distinctions here, however, is that the approach of sports psychologists like Loehr is wholistic—dealing with the whole person, focusing on the whole cycle. Their approach not only sees stress as a positive source of energy, they create training cycles ("wave-making") designed to increase a person's capacity to handle stress ("toughness") by *alternating* between action and stress followed by rest and recovery.

Here's how Loehr describes these ideas in *Toughness Training for Sports:* "To fully understand how stress and recovery relate to the toughening process, we need some working definitions. In the Toughness Training context, stress is anything that causes energy to be expended; recovery is anything that causes energy to be recaptured."

In other words, the whole cycle of stress and recovery is part of the process in sports psychology approach: "Physical stress occurs when you expend energy in moving muscles; mental stress happens when you expend energy in thinking and concentrating; emotional stress comes when you expend energy in feeling fear, anger and other emotions. Physical stess is running a race; mental energy is thinking about race tactics; emotional stress is worrying about how you're going to do in the race."

TRAINING FOR TOUGHNESS
BUILDING ON "WAVES" OF STRESS & RECOVERY

In addition, recovery works at all three levels: "Recovery simply means rest. When you rest, you temporarily break episodes of stress and allow energy to be restored." Physically you get recovery by reducing muscle stimulation. Mentally breaking your concentration and reducing mental stimulation. And you create emotional recovery when you replace negative feelings, such as anger and fear with positive feelings of confidence and calm.

The ideal training is what Loehr calls "wave-making," to increase your toughness to handle stress and enhance performance. The goal is for your coaches and trainers to create an optimum balance between increasing stress and pushing performance to new peaks without overtraining, coupled with periods of recovery to restore energy for the next wave.

Then come successive waves of stress and recovery, reaching for new peaks of performance, new levels of toughness, and in the process increasing a person's capacity to deal with stress—mentally and emotionally as well as physically, a balanced approach to toughening the whole person.

In the short term each sport has its own stess-recovery cycle—tennis may be a ten-second stress mode and a twenty-second recovery.

THE SPORTS/FITNESS ZONE

Golfers spend about ninety-five percent of the time between shots. Football varies with huddles, time-outs, half-times.

But the "critical factor in the big picture—how closely your recovery balances your stress over time." Toughness training sees stress as positive, is designed to build your capacity to handle stress to your advantage. The training focuses on the total person over the long-term in multiple training cycles of stress and recovery, stress and recovery, stress and recovery, ad infinitum .....

THE SPORTS ZONE—MEDITATION IN ACTION

Is this meditation? Absolutely! This is meditation at its best. Even the action-oriented stress phase of the training cycle, although Loehr seems to refer to the recovery phase more as meditation when he breaks down recovery into active and passive forms of recovery: "Active rest includes nonvigorous physical activities that break the cycles of physical, emotional and mental stress."

For a tennis player, active relaxation or meditation could be golf or frisbee. A swimmer might alternate by jogging or biking. A golfer might do yoga, tai chi or fish. Anything to break the cycle. Passive activities also break the cycle: "Laughing, meditation, watching TV or a movie, getting a massage, reading, deep breathing, taking an afternoon nap, having a whirlpool bath." All of them are part of the recovery cycle.

Moreover, throughout Loehr's book and in his organization's Corporate Athlete programs there is considerable use of other meditation techniques in the training of executives and athletes: Visualization of sports programs, positive self-talk and affirmations, body scanning, and focusing on the here-and-now, all designed to increase a person's capacity to handle stress, achieve peak performance and increase productivity.

Bottom line: Fitness training for sports and athletic events—*as well as for recreation and health purposes*—is emerging as the ideal way to meditate because it deals with the whole person, mentally and emotionally as well as physically. Yes, sitting meditation will always be the best way to meditate for certain personalities. However, it is primarily a mental exercise and not enough for action-oriented personalities who seem naturally drawn to the Sports Zone in search of ways to meditate—*and they are finding a lot of them!*

THE SPORTS/FITNESS ZONE

RUNNING, RUNNING, RUNNING
AS MEDITATION

*There is a part of every marathon
where something does take over ...
the sensation of movement ...
You lose a sense of identity in yourself,
you become running itself...
I only have to think of putting on my running shoes
and the kinesthetic pleasure of floating along,
the pleasure of movement starts to come.
I get a feeling of euphoria, almost real happiness ...
It is the platonic idea of knowing thyself.
Running is getting to know yourself
to an extreme degree.
Ian Thompson
world champion
marathoner*

RUNNING HAS LONG been known as a natural meditation for recreational athletes. Then suddenly, a few decades ago, running moved into the spotlight when it also became known as a "positive addiction," thanks to the so-called "runners high," where the runner, the running, and the world move in harmony.

Back in the mid-seventies—about the time the relaxation response and transcentental meditation were emerging as hot topics—noted psychiatrist William Glasser, M.D., author of the bestseller *Reality Therapy,* was working on a research project to determine if people could become addicted to positive behavior.

2.1 RUNNING, RUNNING, RUNNING

RUNNING—AMERICA'S #1 "POSITIVE ADDICTION!"

His research covered a wide range of activities: singing and playing musical instruments, knitting, yoga, exercise, weightlifting, hiking, swimming, cycling, rock climbing—*and running*—which Glasser ultimately concluded is not only America's most common positive addiction, it is also "the hardest but surest way to positive addiction."

Early in his research Dr. Glasser contacted Joe Henderson, editor of *Runner's World* magazine, about his idea that running was a positive addiction. Henderson, a self-admitted eighteen-year running addict, loved the idea and featured Glasser's questionnaire in the magazine.

Glasser's questionnaire asked for detailed information on things like: how long have you been running, how often, competitions, efforts to improve, do you run solo or in groups, how do you deal with discomfort and injuries, any bad habits released, the positive benefits, your state of mind while running, other positive activities, like yoga, music, sports, meditation.

MARATHON CHAMPION
"YOU BECOME RUNNING ITSELF"

Then came the pleasant surprise: Glasser did not expect the avalanche of responses, more than seven hundred arrived. And seventy-five percent of them identified themselves as addicted! The results were published in his book, *Positive Addictions*.

World champion marathoner Ian Thompson best explained why runners become addicted to running. "Runner's high" is actually too nebulous a description. But Thompson talks specifically of the feeling of euphoria and loss of identity, ego and self as you are floating along in the rhythm of the running movement—*"you become running itself!"*—*and that's a perfect meditation!*

RUNNING BEATS TM MEDITATION

In the interview with John Roemer, a 36-year-old marathoner who had been running five-six times a week for over five years, Roemer noted that what he got "from running is almost exactly what the

Maharishi Mahesh Yogi claims would happen if everyone practiced transcendental meditation."

A similar comparison was made by William Bat, who has been running for a couple years. He described his state of mind as "a state of sublimation similar to that experienced during transcendental meditation." But, he added, TM "requires two twenty-minute periods daily and relative privacy, neither of which is easy to find in today's typical lifestyle."

He would rather spend the time running because it is "a period free of mental stress and structured thought, a time to lose myself in nature," said Bat, adding that "several times I have begun my run with the intention of thinking out a problem but this doesn't seem to work for me. I immediately get caught up in the pure and simple act of running." Pure running—*and pure meditation.*

GO INTO THE VOID
NO THINKING, NO CHATTER, JUST PEACE

Glasser's runners clearly prefer running as their meditation rather than any sitting meditation. In fact, so many of the runners described the experience of running in ways you'd expect to hear from monks in sitting meditation—Jim Cory, a runner for eleven years: *"I don't think at all. My awareness is only of the present. Even that cannot be called awareness. Brain chatter is gone."*

And Ronald Rombaski, a 38-year-old businessman, added that while he is running *"my mind is resting in a vacuum ... resting ... not functioning,"* an expression that sounds like 'the void' or ultimate unknowable spirit at the core of 2,500-year-old Taoist bible, the Tao Te Ching, a perfect state of mind for the meditation experience.

BEYOND QUAKER MEDITATION
INTO THE ZEN OF RUNNING

Another wonderful expression of running as a meditation came from Martha Clopfer, a 39-year-old part-time teacher and farmer who had been running five times a week for five years. When asked about her state of mind while running she said: "Meditative is probably the best single word but it is different from Quaker meeting type

2.1 RUNNING, RUNNING, RUNNING

meditation. The most similar state of mind I know comes from listening to music for pleasure."

And like many other runners, Clopfer spoke of becoming one with the flow: "The rhythm of running is a strong element. Sometimes problems get solved while I am running or I think of things to say to people but it is not a figuring out process. More of a sudden flash of insight that comes when you are least trying to find an answer." Once again, that kind of sudden flash of insight reminds us of *satori,* the sudden enlightenment Zen masters experience in za-zen meditation.

MARATHONS, TRIATHLONS, TOUR DE FRANCE

Today you'll find the principles of sports psychology, mental training and moving meditations in virtually every recent book on running and related sports, marathons and triathlons, swimming and cycling, as well as the Tour de France—and usually somewhere in each is a comment like "your mental training is as important as your physical training," plus discussions of other meditation techniques; visualization, focusing, confidence and others.

A few that come to mind are: *Runner's World's Complete Book of Running,* edited by Amby Burfoot, a Boston Marathon winner; *Marathon: The Ultimate Training Guide* by Hal Higdon; *Swim Bike Run* by Hobson, Campbell & Vickers; *Be Iron Fit* by Don Fink a Wall Street investment banker for twenty years before retiring to enter Ironman competitions; and The *Ultimate Ride* by Lance Armstrong's cycling coach, Chris Carmichael.

CHI RUNNING MEDITATION
FOCUS, SCAN, BREATHE, RELAX

One especially intriguing book for runners is Danny Dreyer's *Chi Running.* Danny's a running coach and nationally ranked ultramarathon runner with thirty years experience. Chi-running is a way of training to run effortless and injury-free using four mind/body skills that Dreyer integrated into his running from work with Tai Chi masters.

THE SPORTS/FITNESS ZONE

These four meditation skills are now in common use among sports psychologists and Western stress management clinicians in general as well as with runners, thanks to Dreyer and other professionals like him:

Focusing Your Mind, rather than letting it wander into distractions
Body Sensing: Scanning and listening to your body's signals
Breathing: Tapping into Your Chi. New power through the breath
Relaxation: The Path of Least Resistance. Moving free and loose

Sound familiar? Of course it does. Here are four very familiar techniques and goals we see mentioned over and over in discussions about virtually every one of the popular sitting meditation programs worldwide today.

Except now these techniques are being accepted as an integral part not just of the practice of Tai Chi but of many other moving meditation disciplines such as running. And here we see a great running coach blending these basic meditation skills into the runner's world, and in the process transforming running into a truly effective method of moving meditation.

BLUE JEAN BUDDHA & THE 1,000-DAY MARATHON

A new generation of American Buddhists are also finding their meditation in running. In Sumi Loundon's recent book, *Blue Jean Buddha: Voices of Young Buddhists* we hear David Suniga tell us not only of his experience—well, listen to what he discovered: "My spiritual path as a runner has revealed itself gradually. ... Running naturally lends itself to Buddhist practice; it has been the primary form of meditation for some Japanese and Tibetan orders for over 1,200 years."

"Only a select few of the Japanese Tendai monks of Mount Hiei are allowed to undergo the *sennichi kaihogyo* (1,000-day marathon), which spans seven years. For the first three years, the monks complete a yearly ritual of running 24.8 miles every day for 100 consecutive days ... The Tendai monks believe they can only accomplish their death-defying physical activities because they are following the bodhisattva path. They achieve complete mastery of the minds and bodies for the sake of all sentient beings. By conquering unimaginable physical pain, they are revered as living Buddhas and, like Shakyamuni, prove that dukkha [suffering on earth] can be overcome."

RUNNING—THE ULTIMATE POSITIVE MEDITATION

Dr. Glasser was way ahead of his time. In fact, his unique focus on the *positive* addictive qualities of running and other activities opened the door to the development of sports psychology, while at the same time providing us with a framework for understanding that for many of us running is as powerful and as effective a meditation as practicing Transcendental Meditation, or sitting in silence at a Quaker meeting, or doing za-zen meditation in a Buddhist temple in Japan.

THE SPORTS/FITNESS ZONE

<u>YOGA</u>
AS MEDITATION

*To me, yoga is great physical training,
not something spiritual or religious.
I want to be as effective as I can be in my job.
It's results-driven. And the results are remarkable.*
Bill Gross
Portfolio Manager
Pimco Funds $475 billion

*It's helped me tremendously
flexibility-wise, and
the relaxation techniques calm me down,
which is particularly important on the mound.*
Barry Zito, pitcher
Winner Cy Young Award

BACK IN 1979, Dr. Jon Kabat-Zinn, one of the pioneers in the field of stress management, opened the Stress Reduction Clinic at the University of Massachusetts. In a chapter of his 1990 book, *The Full Catastrophe: Using the Wisdom of Your Body & Mind to Face Stress, Pain & Illness,* Kabat-Zinn offered a strong endorsement of the meditative power of yoga:

"Yoga <u>is</u> meditation ... during slow and gentle strengthening exercises, such as yoga and physical therapy, what people think of traditionally as 'exercise' is transformed into meditation."

The popularity of yoga has grown dramatically in the past decade. Today there are more than 18 million yoga enthusiasts in the United States, compared to an estimated 3 million practicing America Buddhists. Yoga works!

YOGA MEDITATION—TODAY'S NEW SUPER-SPORT

Until recently yoga had an image as a "women's-only club." Today, its popularity has exploded so much it's annoying old-timers who were practicing yoga long before it became super-popular "sport." As Anne Cushman wrote a couple years ago in the *Shambhala Sun*, a Buddhist journal:

"Yoga has gotten to be so impossibly chic, so insanely popular… There are yoga dance clubs, yoga cruises, yoga singles parties; there's disco yoga, aqua yoga, yoga kickboxing. Yoga teachers are the toast of Hollywood parties. Images of sultry young yogis and yoginis sell everything from lingerie to SUVs to luxury apartments in Trump Towers." With women dominating the images.

YES, REAL MEN DO YOGA
ON WALL STREET & THE PITCHER'S MOUND

So when John Capouya's tough-guy book, *Real Men Do Yoga,* hit the bookstores a couple years ago, you could sense that a new wave was already changing, or rather adding to, the American yoga scene.

Capouya's powerful message stands out among the other more traditional books on yoga. Yes, it has the traditional pictures of yoga positions. But what really jumps out at you are the impressive number of personal stories in *Real Men Do Yoga,* profiles from the world of professional sports as well as the real world of business and finance:

—Andy O'Keefe, owner, Wall Street brokerage
—Peter Scirios, architect
—Marty Stein, trade association executive
—Rob Eriksen, real estate developer
—David Cooke, assistant district attorney
—Ted Roman, building contractor
—Jonathan Kelley, restaurateur
—Ken Canfield, trial lawyer

THE SPORTS/FITNESS ZONE

Capouya's book also has many profiles of professional athletes who are dedicated yoga practitioners.

> —Shannon Sharpe, tight end, Denver Broncos
> —Al Leiter, pitcher, New York Mets
> —David Duval, PGA golfer
> —Sean Burke, goaltender, Phoenix Coyotes
> —Eddie George, running back, Tennessee Titans
> —Robby Ginepri, tennis player, ATP Tour
> —Amani Toomer, wide receiver, New York Giants
> —Steve Reed, relief pitcher, Colorado Rockies

These profiles set *Real Men Do Yoga* apart from all the others. And like other yoga books it explains the standard yoga exercises, positions and movements—everything necessary to enjoy the benefits; balance, breathing, flexibility, strength, power, muscular, and energy. Capouya also adds his special recommendations specific to each individual sport.

YOGA TRIGGERS POWERFUL CHANGES IN MEN

Walk into any bookstore and you'll find a large selection of books on the body/mind mechanics of yoga. You can also go online, there are over 30,000 websites devoted to yoga. Either way you'll find all you need to know on the fundamentals. But remember, yoga is an action-oriented meditation, merely reading a book about yoga is no substitute for a good teacher who will give you a head start and get you on the right path.

The basics you can learn; but hearing what a few "real men" have to say about the benefits is convincing evidence that it works! And that just might get you fired up enough to jump in with these real men and start practicing yoga. Here are a few of the powerful testimonials from Capouya's *Real Men Do Yoga:*

ANDY O'KEEFE, WALL STREET BROKER, 44-YEARS-OLD

"I'm married with seven kids. Been on Wall Street for 20 years. I'm the owner of a brokerage form: 110 employees. I'm 6'4", 225 pounds.

2.2 YOGA

I've lifted weights for years and I run. I played lacrosse at college, and basketball, football in high school.

So I love sports. ... I just thought yoga was: you sat there, meditated, stretched. That's all. I thought it a weird Eastern thing. But that's not true at all. ... I feel stronger, more flexible.

And it's helped me with my golf ... Mentally, it kind of clears your head. You can't think about anything, but what you're doing while you're in there. It's a good escape for me."

MARTY STEIN, EXECUTIVE, 53-YEARS-OLD

"In 1997, I was having some really nagging back problems. I was playing golf 3 to 4 times a week, and in order to play, I had to take 6 to 8 Advils—two before, two at the turn, and two after—and I was wearing back braces for support ...

A masseuse convinced me to try yoga, and I went to around three classes per week and tried to do some every day and night at home. I immediately noticed a difference. I didn't put on the brace or take Advil, and at the end of the day I felt fine ...

It has a calming effect. I also realize that if I was in my car and got cut off, a couple of yoga breaths helped me from getting road rage and to just relax—it works in other areas of my life, too."

PETER SCIRIOS, ARCHITECT, 47-YEARS-OLD

"I played semi-pro rugby for years—and yoga was the result. I was having a lot of problems with my neck and my knees, and I was taking 6 to 8 ibuprofen a day. Yoga was purely therapeutic; I gradually got myself off the painkillers and could walk normally again ...

I think yoga allowed me to continue the things I enjoy—basketball, windsurfing, biking. I can keep up with guys 10 to 15 years younger than me. My body shape has changed drastically but I feel just as strong as I was. I have more endurance and weigh 30 pounds less.

Also, I've been an architect for 20 years and I was struggling with the beginnings of carpal tunnel syndrome from all the computer work and leaning over, and I have overcome that with yoga."

If these guys haven't sold you, wait and let the message sink in. At least buy *Real Men Do Yoga* and read the whole book so you got the whole picture. When the timing is right you'll know in your gut if yoga is right for you, and whether this kind of moving meditation can make your life fuller—as physical exercise, preventative medicine, psychological balance and an uplifted spirit.

WARNING: ADDICTIVE, AGELESS, ALIVE!

The rapid growth in yoga's popularity is also due to the fact that it works so well as a basic exercise routine, without any religious overtones. In fact, Capouya confirms yoga's secular emphasis by dealing with it in a casual throw-away line: "As for the spiritual thing, that's up to you."

But watch out, it may sneak in the backdoor anyway, without you even realizing it says Beth Shaw in the *Los Angeles Times:* "To do yoga and say you're not getting the spiritual is like saying 'I'm drinking milk but I'm not getting calcium.' Spirituality is inherent in the practice."

So don't be surprised if yoga quietly reveals a new earthy spirituality within you at a deeper personal level, one that touches all of nature and is in tune with a universal force everywhere—an awesome power that you may well choose to keep private because words are inadequate to describe it.

One final note from Capouya's encouraging, life-changing book: "Some of these men laughingly call themselves yoga addicts, and swear they'll practice it for the rest of their lives. That's another yoga advantage: You're never too old to do it, enjoy it and benefit from it. More good news: You can start to see all the results in just two hours a week."

And you thought meditation was for wimps? Not in the yoga-jock club!

2.3 TENNIS

TENNIS
AS MEDITATION

> *The final stage of mental toughness is*
> *reflected in the challenge response.*
> *You actually find yourself investing more positive intensity,*
> *more of yourself as the situation gets tougher.*
> *You find that problems you face in competition are not threatening*
> *but stimulating. You've gone well beyond simply loving to win.*
> *You have clearly come to love the battle.*
> *As a result of this emotional response, you have*
> *become an excellent problem solver. When everyone else*
> *is heading for the trenches as the problems start mounting,*
> *you smile inside because you know*
> *you got the emotional edge.*
> James Loehr
> The Mental Game
> Winning at Pressure Tennis

AT FIRST GLANCE, you might think that tennis is anything but meditation. Unlike other moving meditations—such as Tai Chi, Yoga, surfing, fly fishing and backpacking, which are gentle, moving you into a peaceful space—tennis is intense, relentlessly pushing you high up the stress gauge. Just watching a tennis match is stressful. There seems no time for meditation during a match, at least not the traditional image of sitting meditation that comes to mind.

THE SPORTS/FITNESS ZONE

CHAMPIONS MEDITATE WHILE PLAYING THE WORLD'S MOST STRESSFUL SPORT

True, there is no doubt that the game of tennis is extremely stressful. In fact, in *The Mental Game: Winning at Pressure Tennis* Jim Loehr compares tennis to every other sport he's ever worked in the prior decade—hockey, basketball, football, soccer, gymnastics, figure skating, golf, swimming, running, boxing—and he says that without question in all his years as a sports psychologist "tennis is the toughest of all from an emotional perspective."

Why is tennis the toughest on the stress scale? Many factors pile on top of one another to make tennis a pressure-cooker: No substitutions, no time-outs, no coaching, exhausting no-time-limit games, a scoring system that keeps the pressure on, unpredictable and nervewracking courts and playing conditions, constant fan scrutiny, an aggressive in-your-face opponent out to beat you, plus your self-esteem is on the line, especially if you're a professional player.

ACTIVE MEDITATIONS MANAGE HIGH STRESS

Tennis is the ultimate high-stress sport, and the only way for a player to get to the top of their game is to find ways to manage the relentless stress, and the new world of meditation offers solutions that work. So where are all these hidden opportunities to meditate during a tennis match? Here are the key ones:

— **Between the points** (recovery phase, or the relaxation response).
— **During the volley and rally** (focus and concentration).
— **Reduction of emotional intensity** (breath control).
— **Before the game** (visualization and affirmations).
— **Increasing your capacity to handle stress** (training goals)

Today's new meditation teachers understand how to work with athletes in all sports. Moreover, these new teachers no longer come from the ranks of traditional mind/body clinicians and Far Eastern spiritual leaders who may be biased toward their heritage. Rather, the new ones are more likely to sport a stop watch, wear Nikes, hi-fashion wraparound sunglasses and a baseball cap.

2.3 TENNIS

SPORTS PSYCHOLOGISTS
A NEW BREED OF MEDITATION GURUS

The new breed of meditation teachers are sports psychologists, athletic trainers, team coaches, physical therapists, and other sports medicine experts. These guys understand and appreciate the value of meditation from first-hand experience. They use many the same basic techniques as their predecessors but they adapt them for action-oriented clients. In addition, they're able to integrate simple meditation skills into the bigger training picture without getting caught up in all the ritual and mystique of traditionalists in the field of meditation.

The fact is, sports psychologists see tennis from a totally different vantage point. In their minds—as experts dedicated to helping players reduce stress and increase performance—not only is tennis a perfect opportunity for meditation, these sports psychologists have researched the great tennis players and seen how they have *instinctively mastered the art of meditating during the game in the middle of the action*—and that's the key to their success.

TOUGHNESS TRAINING
BALANCING STRESS & RECOVERY

Today's sports training professionals know that athletes not only can learn these meditation techniques and put them into action as part of a total training program—now universally known as "toughness training"—they know tennis players *have to learn these simple tools if they want to win at pressure tennis!*

In a *Success* magazine interview of Loehr and his partner, Jack Groppel, author of *The Corporate Athlete,* "toughness" is described as "the ability to perform at your peak when the stress is highest."

"That peak is what athletes call zoning," says Loehr. When you're in the zone, "you're very energized, relaxed, and calm inside but with a tremendous sense of confidence, intensity, and alertness. Zoning occurs in the Ideal Performance State (IPS), a special climate of mental, physical and emotional toughness."

THE SPORTS/FITNESS ZONE

MEDITATING "IN THE ZONE"

When you're "in the zone" everything comes together as moments of intense competition and peak performance flow naturally and effortlessly in rhythm with periods of relaxation and recovery. "The key is to structure episodes of stress," says Loehr. "You perform in waves. You cannot be at your best all the time, so you have to pick your times of recovery as carefully as you pick your peak times."

That's it, a simple stress management training for tennis players based on a simple concept alternating between stress and relaxation. You build your capacity to handle stress so you can perform at your peak under stress. And secondly, as part of your training, you also learn how to modulate periods of peak performance with recovery cycles—rest, relaxation, and recovery during brief periods of meditation.

RECOVERING BETWEEN POINTS
WORLD'S FASTEST 16-SECOND MEDITATION

In *The Mental Game,* Loehr describes in considerable detail how the top competitors recover "between the points"—after the stress of the serve and volley. His conclusions summarize years of personal interviews, analysis of game tapes and other studies using biofeedback instruments and heart monitoring devices: "I've discovered that top competitors typically complete four rather distinct patterns of activity. Players with competitive problems, however, invariably fail to complete one or more of these activities."

Here is the ultimate meditation cycle used by top competitors during the intense heat of the game. Understanding this cycle is crucial to understanding how truly effective periods of meditation are possible in very brief moments—not only in tennis, but in virtually any business setting, including the middle of a tense deal negotiation where you often have just a few seconds to spare.

Stage one. The Positive Physical Response.

The instant the point ends, switch hands with the racket and take actions that create positive emotions. If you won the point, pump the arm. If not, do something to reduce frustrations and anger, such

2.3 TENNIS

as turning your back on the mistake and let it go. Walk tall, walk confident. All in 3-5 seconds.

Stage two. The Relaxation Response.

You might call this an essential mini-version of Dr. Benson's "relaxation response." It lasts roughly 6 to 15 seconds. Continue the post-point high-energy walk, gradually slowing down. Focus on the racket or ground, collect yourself. Take a moment to scan the body. Focus solely on getting calm and relaxing, stretch a bit and take control of your breathing cycle.

Stage three. The Preparation Response.

Now 3-5 seconds to move back into concentration. "You're programming your computer." Check the score as you re-engage your mind. Know what you intend to do before the next point starts. If serving, take command. You might verbalize the score, staring straight at your opponent. Own the court. By your actions and inner dialogue, affirm that you're confident you'll win this point.

Stage four. The Automatic Ritual Response.

Before the serve, top competitors take 5-8 seconds to go through a sequence of automatic physical movements in order to create the highest state of mental and physical readiness for the intensity of the next point. The server might bounce the ball two, three times, then pause, visualize where the serve is going. On the return, the player's ritual may be swaying, jumping around, spinning the racket, blowing on their hands. Focus and concentrate.

And with this slow-motion version of the ultra-fast 16-second recovery phase "in the zone," we get a review of every major meditation technique in existence used by today's top athletes in the tennis game—*focusing, staying in the moment, breath control, visualization, affirmations, body scanning, concentration, and the relaxation response*. In slow-motion we see the best meditations offered throughout history—*in brief 16-second action clips.*

THE SPORTS/FITNESS ZONE

YOU ARE MEDITATING 20 MINUTES DURING EVERY MATCH

And that's it. There's no twenty minutes of meditation at one stretch. Yet in a long match all the 16-second intervals occurring between the stress cycle and the recovery cycle easily add up to more than a total of twenty minutes in a tennis game. So it is essential that these precious moments "between the points" be used wisely. *In fact, if you want to increase your capacity to handle stress and win at pressure tennis—and in life—you have no choice!*

2.4 GOLF

GOLF
AS MEDITATION

*When Mitchell and I first spoke, he remarked,
'The spiritual stuff you think about is something
I frequently experience on the golf course.
I wish I could experience it when I'm not playing golf.'
I responded, 'That's how I feel most of the time,
but I lose it when I play golf.'
We made a deal. I would teach Mitchell the rules that
make the game of life a joyful, ecstatic expression.
Mitchell would teach me the rules that make the
game of golf a joyful, ecstatic experience.
Guess what. They are the same rules.*
Deepak Chopra
The A.I.M. of Golf

GOLF IS THE perfect meditation for millions of Americans—great exercise, you're enjoying nature outdoors, intense mental training, and an intangible spiritual experience. Jack Nicklaus's "ability to focus intensely on whatever I'm doing through most distractions" is an exactly the same lesson every meditation master practices and teaches, whether in an Eastern monastery or Western stress management clinic. It's all the same.

Of course, a golf master like Jack Nicklaus would probably hesitate to compare what he does so naturally with the meditation practices of a great spiritual leader like the Dalai Lama. Although the word meditation may not be a familiar term in golf manuals and digests, we definitely sense the spirit and spirituality inherent in golf whenever golf is discussed.

FINDING YOUR SOUL
IN THE SWING AND "IN BETWEEN"

One delightful early classic is *Golf in the Kingdom,* Michael Murphy's mystical tale about a young man headed for India in the fifties, headed off to study metaphysics and meditation at guru Sri Aurobindo's ashram. But first he stops in Scotland to play at the legendary Burningbush golf club. That day his life is transformed as he is paired with a mysterious golf teacher named Shivas Irons who reveals the simple secrets of life through the metaphor of golf:

"Yes, a man's style o' play and his swing certainly reflects the state of his soul," Shivas told the young traveler. As do the moments in between, while you're on the path to the next hole: "If ye can enjoy the walkin', ye can probably enjoy the other times in yer life when ye're *in between.* And that's most o' the time; wouldn't ye say?"

The "in between" times then become a different kind of meditation, a relaxed walking meditation. Nicklaus put it in even simpler, natural terms, "unless the tee shot finds serious trouble, when I might immediately start processing possible recoveries, I descend into a valley as I leave the tee, either through casual conversation with a fellow competitor or by letting my mind dwell on whatever happens into it."

GOLF ENLIGHTENS THE LAST SAMURAI

We heard the same spirit from Ken Watanabe, the Oscar-nominated Japanese actor who played Katsumoto, the samurai leader in *The Last Samurai.* When Watanabe first took up golf his endless mistakes often keep him awake at night, ruminating:

"Now I have a change of mind. When I was reading a book about golf, I found a great word for my new attitude: 'Same walk, same smile.' If you keep up your pace of how you walk through 18 holes and don't forget to smile the whole time, you can get a good score. It's like life and like work, movie work and acting work. It's the same. Every day's okay. No problem." And in this profoundly simple awareness Watanabe is as enlightened as the Dalai Lama.

It is all the same—in work or play, golf or life—it's all in how you play the game, in the swing or in-between. The game of golf, this meditation, your life, the spirit world are there in all—*in the swing and in between*—in an endless cycle of change and continuity as you "move from peaks of concentration to valleys of relaxation and back again as necessary."

ZEN GOLFER'S KOAN
"YOU AND BALL ARE ONE!"

We see it in the prolific best-selling author Dr. Deepak Chopra who shortly after taking up the game found a powerful new level of spirituality that he described with the passion of a born-again evangelist. In *Golf for Enlightenment* Chopra applies the lessons learned in golf to the game of life in a way paralleling his other works, such as *Creating Affluence, Quantum Healing, Perfect Health* and *The Seven Spiritual Laws of Success.*

Seasoned golfers may smile at Chopra's ultra-simple maxims ("you and the ball are one") but his followers and other newcomers to the game will relish the simplicity, especially from a mind-body guru whose enthusiasm clearly confirms the spiritual and meditative power inherent in playing golf.

Similarly, M. Scott Peck's *Golf and The Spirit* shares with us the spiritual journey of this celebrated psychiatrist, the author of the best-selling self-help book, *The Road Less Traveled.* Peck offers yet another perspective on golf as a metaphor for living, with lessons reminiscent of *The Road* books.

THE TAO OF THE GAME—IN SIX LESSONS

After Peck's powerful reminder that we can "stay in the flow only when we get ourselves out of the way, only when we are empty enough to let the Tao (or the divine) flow through us," he offers this beautiful summary of his six lessons for winning at the game of golf, and the game of life:

THE SPORTS/FITNESS ZONE

> *Be attentive to the hazards ahead of you, but empty yourself of your fear of them.*
> *Strive to do your best, but empty yourself of your concern with your score.*
> *Learn from every mistake, but empty yourself of any shred of self-hatred for your imperfections.*
> *Compete, but empty yourself of shame from not measuring up.*
> *Play to win, but if you fail to do so, empty yourself of any remorse.*
> *Remember, every good thing you have been taught, but in that fraction of a second when your clubhead is connecting with the ball, empty yourself of all your remembering.*

Although neither of these guru-doctors are on the PGA money tour, they clearly speak of the game in such reverential tones that everyone knows deep-down that golf is indeed a spiritual experience—something every golfer knows instinctively.

THE "AUTHENTIC SWING" IS WITHIN YOU

And who could forget *The Legend of Bagger Vance*, the story of a haunted war hero who had long been searching the world for the meaning of his WWI trauma. He is drawn into a mythical match between golf greats Bobby Jones and Walter Hagen. And in that fateful game the hero's caddy and spiritual guide, Vance, helps him find his 'Authentic Swing,' and the doorway to his inner self.

The intense bond between golfers and their game is both fascinating and a source of envy. They have clearly found something special—*they seem to be on a strange spiritual path searching for, and finding, something special while playing the game of golf.* And isn't that search what life is all about?

All my life I have been surrounded by guys in this unique society—on both sides of my family and among my friends everywhere in my community. And periodically I'll read in *Forbes*, *Fortune* or *Business Week*, for example, telling us that on top of all the other benefits, golf is great for business contacts.

You can feel their love the game and see how it is working in their life. For them the game of golf is clearly an experience that helps make them whole persons, physically, mentally, emotionally

2.4 GOLF

and spiritually. And yet, if you get into a clubhouse conversation, it is more likely to center on handicaps, clubs, swings, pros, tours, foursomes, tournaments, macho jokes, and how well so-and-so is doing ... not about God, meditation and spiritual experiences.

THE GOLFERS' SHARED SECRET
ONE THAT MONKS TAKE YEARS TO FIND

But I sense that's more because the metaphysical world of golf is so very personal that it's hard to put into words. Just as most golfers aren't on the pro tour, they're also handicapped when it comes to talking and writing about golf as a spiritual experience or meditation tool. So that task is left to a Chopra, Peck or Nicklaus, someone who understands the game and has the gift of words too.

Still, most golfers share the secret—that golfers have already found what monks spend decades searching for in sitting meditation. Maybe monks should get out of the monastery for a while. What they're looking for is right there waiting for them at the club, on the course, in the incredible game of golf.

GOLF, THE ULTIMATE MEDITATION

And they reach this enlightenment with a very simply meditation used over and over on an 18-hole course—although they don't use the words meditation and enlightenment to describe the experience.

Here's how Jack Nicklaus described this simple meditation in *Golf My Way:* "First I 'see' the ball where I want it to finish, nice and white and sitting high on the bright grass. Then the scene quickly changes and I 'see' the ball going there: its path, trajectory, and shape, even its behavior on landing. Then there is a sort of fade out, and the next scene shows me making the kind of swing that will turn the previous images into reality."

This golf meditation beats counting your breaths, mantras, chanting, and while your handicap may not drop enough to put you on the pro golf tour it can be as effective as spending years in a Tibetan monastery—well, at least more fun—if you want to achieve the golfer's unique enlightenment.

WALKING, HIKING & CLIMBING
AS MEDITATION

Our true home is the present moment.
The miracle is not to walk on water.
The miracle is to walk on the green earth
in the present moment.
Peace is all around us—in the world and in nature
and within us—in our bodies and our spirits.
Thich Nhat Hanh
Living Buddha, Living Christ

MY GRANDPARENTS RAISED me. Grandpa loved gardening, which was a good thing, we lived off his harvest. He was a gentle soul with a big heart and strong values. He walked the way he talked, with integrity. He was a great example. Today when anyone tells a story about their grandfather, my ears perk up and I smile, reminded of my youth. I felt especially warm reading this one by a well-known meditation teacher whose grandfather taught her a important lesson—*that meditation is something we all do, naturally, without thinking.*

GRANDPA TEACHES MEDITATION GURU THE BIG SECRET

"I visited my grandfather when he was very, very old," says Sylvia Boornstein in *It's Easier Than You Think: The Buddhist Way to Happiness.* "Twice a day, after breakfast and lunch, he would invite me to accompany him on a walk around the block. It was a long

2.5 WALKING, HIKING & CLIMBING

walk, because he walked slowly. He explained to me that this was his regular regimen, his daily exercise."

Then came the sudden ah-ha to this young psychotherapist, "I said to him, 'what do you think about when you walk?' He looked at me in surprise. 'What do you mean, what do I think about?' he asked. 'When I walk, I walk!' By that time I thought he was a Buddha." Maybe all granddads are, mine sure was.

HE WALKS LIKE A BUDDHA BECAUSE HE IS ONE

Is walking meditation really *that* simple? Yes! When you walk, you just walk. I guess it just takes time to grasp the simplicity of meditation, and life in general! Maybe all grandfathers are enlightened because they've walked around the block a few more times than we have. They get it, and I guess that's what makes them great buddies as well as Buddhas.

Walking with them helps us see as they see. And if you're lucky, you'll get it too. In getting the deeper meaning of her grandfather's simple remark, this meditation teacher saw something about herself. She saw that he really was enlightened—and in that, she was also enlightened in that moment! Isn't that what meditation is all about!

Walking is so natural, yet so easily ignored in the rush of the daily work commute. Walking slows you down. Get out of your car, feel the world around you, see the colors, smell the roses—and as you walk, look inside at how wonderful you are.

Walking is exercise for many of us, an opportunity to get in touch with ourselves and with others. It is a way of communion with the divine for others. As the American naturalist Henry Thoreau walked the trails of his beloved Walden Pond he say "heaven is under our feet as well as over our heads."

WILDERNESS BACKPACKING THE "MOST PROFOUND MEDITATION"

Every hiker, every climber, every trail blazer, every backpacker on a long trek is a modern day Thoreau. I stumbled on this message unexpectedly in Ryel Kestenbaun's *The Ultralight Backpacker,* an outdoorsman whose entire life is a meditation. Listen to his magical way of drawing you onto the path with him:

"In daily life, there is precious little time to let our minds rest quietly. Our brains are so used to being fed a constant diet of stimulation that we find it difficult to engage in the practice of doing nothing. The interesting thing about cutting off that stimulation for a little while is what remains behind. Rather than our minds becoming an empty box, they become conduits for the myriad of thoughts, emotions, and celebrations that never had a chance to flow before. That is one of the gifts of meditation."

Suddenly he shifts from giving you expert backpacking advice—on stuff like tents, tarps, sleeping bags and boots—to letting you into the big secret he has discovered walking in nature: "You can practice meditation anywhere, at any time—sitting in your car at a red light, eating dinner at a restaurant, and yes, backpacking along a trail. The *most profound meditative states* I've ever reached came while walking by myself along a trail deep in the backcountry, immersed completely in the world around me *and* within my own self."

NATURE—THE BEST MEDITATION TEMPLE

My spine tingled when I read Kestenbaun, our favorite backpacker, speaking in pure Thoreau imagery. Listen: "Nature is one giant meditation room. Whether you are striding along a rugged trail beneath a canopy of dense pines, or sitting on a giant granite rock overlooking a glass-smooth lake, or standing high up on a lonesome peak with a view that stretches to infinity, nature provides us with an opportunity to turn down the volume of our everyday lives and become utterly connected with who we truly are. I don't think I've ever taken a single trip to the wilderness without coming back feeling more aware of myself and appreciative of the people and the world around me."

Back in the eighties I spent a month at Esalen Institute in the Big Sur hiking the Coastal Sierras with Steve Harper, an Outward Bound instructor. Steve knew every inch of the trails in those rugged mountains.

2.5 WALKING, HIKING & CLIMBING

On one hike he took us way up to an 800-year-old village site of the Esalen Indians. There we saw mounds of mussel shells that they had carried up from the Pacific Ocean shores hundreds of feet below. Their culture disappeared with almost no trace. Why? You think of those kinds of things while you're walking slowly through the greatest meditation temple of all.

SITTING IS PENANCE
WALKING IS PURE GRACE

While at Esalen I had a chance to hear Sam Keen, a popular speaker on philosophy, relationships and men's issues. Keen is a former editor of *Psychology Today,* and was featured in a Bill Moyers PBS special, "Your Mythic Journey." In Keen's *Hymns to an Unknown God: Awakening the Spirit in Everyday Life* he speaks poetically of his love of walking meditation:

"For me, sitting meditation, like repentance, is *work* that requires a sizeable amount of concentration, soul-searching, and willpower. Walking, by contrast, is pure *grace,* an effortless art that produces surprising moments of spontaneous self-transcendence. When I walk, my mind leaps ahead, skips steps, and presents me with images and ideas out of nowhere. With surprising regularity the thoughts that come to me when I am on a long hike in the hills contain the breakthrough insights I have been unable to reach after weeks of hard intellectual or emotional work."

Who could ask for anything more! Yes, walking is the perfect meditation. And fortunately, like breathing, we're doing it all the time anyway, so it is the perfect time to meditate every day!

Healthy exercise, trailblazing, a journey through history, communion with nature, delightful sounds, colors and images, birds, flowers, a little soul-searching, conscious contact with the mysterious creator of the universe, and a chance to turn off all the endless distractions of everyday life. That's walking meditation—*the way to your soul.*

THE SPORTS/FITNESS ZONE

THE SPORT CLIMBER'S "MENTAL EDGE"

Many outdoorsmen prefer the challenges of mountain climbing and rock climbing, as a way of meditating on nature and the soul at the same time. In fact, deeply religious Sherpas, Tibetan Buddhists from Nepal, make their living as guides for climbers on their journey up Mt. Everest.

The sport of rock climbing is closer to home and more widely practiced. As its popularity grows, rock climbers are also turning to sports psychologists and sports training techniques to enhance their performance. Goddard & Neumann's *Performance Rock Climbing* emphasizes the basic meditation techniques of breathing, muscle relaxation and concentration, complete with a sketch of a climber in the lotus position to emphasize concentration!

John Long's *Sport Climbing* adds that psychological and behavioral preparation are as essential as physical preparation, not just for survival, but for peak performance:

"Take two climbers of the same ability and fitness. The one with the 'right head' will prove the superior climber every time. She's the one who knows how to program her mind for performance. She may do this through imaging, visualization, self-hypnosis, relaxation techniques, and a host of other methods ... all of which long have been used by athletes to gain some mental edge."

In short, the sport of climbing has become yet another great way of meditating. As Long puts it: "The biggest weapon we have in our quest for peak performance is our mind."

THE MARTIAL ARTS
AS MEDITATION

> *"Your mind is not here," he said.*
> *I made no effort to deny he was right;*
> *students of martial arts soon learn that their teachers*
> *can see right through them. Standing there on the*
> *hard ground in Korea, I just bowed my head slightly*
> *and waited for Mr. Shin to continue.*
> *"What you are doing at the moment*
> *must be exactly what you are doing*
> *at the moment—and nothing else" ...*
> *Mr. Shin's advice, my first lesson in Zen,*
> *came back to me again and again*
> *during my years as a competitor.*
> Chuck Norris
> *The Secret Power Within*

THE ENTERTAINMENT INDUSTRY has popularized the martial arts and captured the hearts and minds of Americans in recent years with films like *The Matrix*, *Crouching Tiger, Hidden Dragon*, and *The Last Samurai*. And before them, the works of Bruce Lee and David Carradine were cult classics. Yet, our fascination goes further back than the dazzling high-tech computer images in contemporary films, back centuries to ancient Japan and the Samurai warriors.

INTO THE SOUL OF THE WARRIOR

The Samurai tradition is often called the 'Soul of Japan' because it reflects the ancient spirit of the great warriors of the East in a way

THE SPORTS/FITNESS ZONE

paralleling the tradition of the Knights of King Arthur's Roundtable in Western culture. Around 1700, after five centuries of military rule, a Confucian scholar and military strategist, Shigesuke, wrote *Bushido for Beginners,* a code of honor as well as a training manual for new Samurais.

Today the principles in the Bushido Code are deeply engrained in the Japanese psyche and culture, extending far beyond the written rules, beyond military strategies, swordsmanship and death. The code speaks to the warrior's entire way of life, to the duties of loyalty owed to family and shogun, service to society, to a way of life grounded in discipline, ethical conduct and personal honor. And fortunately, the code lives on today in the martial arts.

FOCUS ON WHAT YOU ARE DOING RIGHT NOW
NOTHING ELSE

"Your mind is not here," said Jae Chul Shin, Chuck Norris' martial arts master, after noticing that Norris had been slacking off after earning his black belt. And with that gentle admonition, Norris, who later went on to become a world champion in the martial arts, got "his first lesson in Zen, without even knowing it." Zen teaching often sneaks up on us silently.

In that one crucial moment as the master made his point, the student learned the power of the thousand-year tradition of the Code of the Bushido, the Way of the Samurai Warrior and all martial arts, the heart of Zen meditation as well as the ultimate secret of success for contemporary business men and women—all into one profoundly simple principle:

"What you are doing at the moment must be exactly what you are doing at the moment—and nothing else. There is no control when the mind is absent. You must be one with yourself and with what you are doing. While doing something, you are doing it to the fullest. That is true Zen."

True Zen? Yes, the martial arts, Zen and meditation are all one and the same for *the literal translation of the word Zen is "meditation,"* although historically and culturally it does not mean meditation in the usual sense. In fact, Westerns often see the Zen experience as a

2.6 THE MARTIAL ARTS

bunch of obscure and contradictory messages. And yet, Zen, like all of life, is profoundly simple.

ZEN MASTER—"GET TO THE BOTTOM LINE!"

"Although many people don't realize it, Zen is not about monks meditating as much as it is about taking action and making decisive moves in the present," says Norris. "There's a certain impatience about Zen, an unwillingness to get lost in meandering arguments, a desire to cut quickly to the essential, or to 'get to the bottom line'."

Whether in the martial arts or in the business world, Zen is very, very simple to understand—get to the bottom line, and that means you: "Zen wants you to find yourself. Zen actively wants you to achieve happiness and be content with your life." Ultimately then, as in all wisdom traditions throughout history, the goal is finding yourself.

And whether practicing the martial arts, or meditating, or getting to the bottom line in a business deal, the ball is forever being tossed back in your court because "one of the basic tenets of Zen is that it really has nothing to teach, nothing to say," says Norris. "According to Zen the truth is obvious, or should be. The truth is nothing that can be taught ... instead, you have to become aware of it on your own." You are responsible.

THE SECRET POWER OF MARTIAL ARTS IN THE BUSINESS WORLD

Although my experience in the martial arts is limited, I have been a student of Zen for over three decades as well as an observer of the power martial arts bring to a person's life. Chuck Norris' *The Secret Power Within: Zen Solutions for Real Problems* offers perhaps the single best explanation of the history, tradition and meaning of Zen and its role in the martial arts because it speaks directly to today's business executives in their own language. In fact, Norris has been a great teacher in both arenas.

Here's a hard-nosed no-nonsense action-oriented businessman who learned how to get to the bottom line both as a world-class martial arts champion and a major star of film and television, and

THE SPORTS/FITNESS ZONE

also in the school of hard knocks where he had to rebuild a successful national franchise business following a partner's embezzlement that nearly drove him into bankruptcy.

The martial arts are already widely practiced as active meditation for millions of Americans. It is great physical exercise, it sharpens the mind's ability to focus, it does encourage a sense of well-being and reduce stress, plus the Zen philosophy is a perfect way to business success. And yes, you may also want to try Norris' approach to passive meditation:

"There are very precise rules for meditation, but since not everyone has the time, or even the ability to perform them, they can be modified, even to the point where they are no longer related to the basic rules ... it is the content of Zen meditation that matters, not the style or the trappings."

SHUT OUT THE WORLD, WAKE UP THE MIND

In other words, you develop a style that fits you personally, rather than following the ritualistic format of some popular guru. In his case "the key to meditation begins with breath control. I first became acquainted with controlling my breathing when I was studying martial arts in Korea."

Norris prefers starting before sunrise with a basic sitting meditation in his workout room. He faces a blank wall in the familiar cross-legged position. Nothing out of the ordinary. As the meditation progresses "in time you will ignore your breathing as it finds its own rhythm, at which point the outside world will be shut out and the inside world will begin to wake up. It is only then that I try to concentrate on a pleasant image or a phrase or problem. The answer to a problem begins with seeing that it is really in my mind, and not something external."

MEDITATION SHARPENS THE DECISION-MAKER

As you might well expect, Norris' way of meditation is also a key asset for him in the business world: "As an actor-producer-writer of my own films and television series, I am often confronted with situations involving many people, some of them angry, belligerent, or

2.6 THE MARTIAL ARTS

defensive, and everyone looking to me for a solution to the problem. When that happens, I control my breathing, and it always restores calm, confidence, and strength. It allows me to bring my emotions and thoughts under control, so that I can focus on what's at hand."

Today many business men and women practice the martial arts along with za-zen meditation. Norris tells their story: "For me the act of meditation is the act of clearing and calming my mind. I am not in a monastery. I am a contemporary man living a full life, and Zen is part of my life, not a replacement for it."

In the final analysis, we learn that life itself is the ultimate meditation. If you are living a full life, you will find out who you are, something no one can do for you—not Zen, not meditation, not martial arts, not a great master, only you. They may help, but only you will ever know for sure, by living your life fully.

So remember: "What you are doing at the moment must be *exactly* what you are doing at the moment—and nothing else."

THE SPORTS/FITNESS ZONE

TAI CHI
AS MEDITATION

*For some, the flowing,
slowly unfolding form of tai chi is
more suitable for meditation than sitting in one place.
Still others consider a moving meditation highly satisfying
philosophically because they believe everything in the universe
is constantly in motion and they can harmonize best with
the universe through meditation that also moves ...
whatever a student's reason for meditation,
whether stemming from a desire for relief
from the mental tension to a longing for
some form of spiritual enlightenment,
engaging in tai chi can have a
number of mind-quieting and
mind expanding results.*
Herman Kaus
*Tai Chi Handbook: Exercise,
Meditation & Self Defense*

THE MARTIAL ARTS such as Karate, Judo and Tai Kwan Do, rely on the more aggressive Yang energy that we also see reflected in the Bushido code of Japanese Samurai warriors. In contrast, Tai Chi emerges from the wisdom of ancient China and its 2,500-year-old Taoist tradition and taps into the gentler Yin, receptive energy. TaoSports is a modern merger of this ancient tradition with today's world of competitive athletics and physical fitness. Years ago I had an opportunity to study briefly under one of the best.

2.7 TAI CHI

Chungliang Al Huang, one of the world's great Chinese Tai Chi masters teamed up with American sports psychologist Jerry Lynch to describe this modern adaptation in two books: *Thinking Body, Dancing Mind: TaoSports for Extraordinary Performance in Athletics, Business, and Life,* and *Working Out, Working Within: The Tao of Inner Fitness Through Sports & Exercise.* At their core, however, both traditions—*Zen and Taoism*—have the same goals, discovery of your true self and harmonizing your energy with the forces of nature.

LEARNING "TAOSPORTS" FROM THE MASTER

It was my good fortune to be at the Esalen Institute in the Big Sur when Al Huang stopped in for a weekend. Huang is the founder of the Lan Ling Institute in China and the Living Tao Foundation in America. What luck, to have the essence of Tai Chi and the Tao passed on from such a master. Later when I did read his works, everything made sense, all the pieces fell into place naturally.

That was the late eighties. I was exhausted from several years in a high-pressured consulting practice in Los Angeles and decided to take a three-month sabbatical as an Esalen work scholar, where I could heal and recoup my strength relaxing in their soothing hot springs tubs, hike inland through the mountains and work on their farm. I had been there many times for weekend seminars but this was a new opportunity for an extended stay.

A GREAT MEDITATION HALL— WORKING A FARM

If you love the outdoors, the Esalen farm has got to be one of nature's most perfect meditation halls, better than being in any of the world's great temples and cathedrals. Monks know. It sure felt that way every day for me.

Situated on a bluff high above the water's edge, you work the land with one eye looking out over the majestic Pacific Ocean out to the horizon, and behind you the redwood forests of the Coastal Sierra range climb high into the sky. The fresh smells of sea and earth touch the soul like incense.

THE SPORTS/FITNESS ZONE

The labors of the day were simple farm chores, doing whatever needed to be done to get food to the kitchen for three daily meals—*picking corn, planting carrots, mixing fertilizer, driving their mini-tractor, setting up the irrigation system, or hauling garbage from the mess hall to the compost yard*—and whatever you did was an endless meditation.

In the Esalen world your work and your whole life naturally becomes meditation, all day, every day. If Thoreau had ever visited Esalen he would have called it Walden Pond West, for in both places "heaven is under our feet as well as over our heads."

YOU ARE ALWAYS ONE WITH THE TAO
TRUST IT, TRUST YOURSELF

The dining lodge is short walk south of the farm, with a similar expansive view high above the ocean. At the edge of the bluff, some six hundred feet above the ocean, there is a large observation deck. It was there that Al Huang gave us the greatest lesson of Tai Chi: *Your body already knows how to move all by itself, it is in your nature, you are at one with the Tao, trust your Chi and move with it.*

We had been expecting the master to demonstrate the basic moves of the traditional Tai Chi forms that have guided its practitioners for thousands of years—*grasp the bird's tail, sweep the table, single whip, wave hands like clouds, listen to seashell, repulse the monkey, figure eight, fair lady weaves shuttles*—but that was not master Al Huang's message. He was in the ancient tradition of passing wisdom through example and experience, and going to the essence of the Tao.

THE SOUL OF TAI CHI IS
FLOWING IN THE GOLDEN LIGHT

He wanted to center us immediately within the heart and soul of Tai Chi. What is it? Tai Chi is not found in rituals, not in some externally prescribed set of body movements, with masses of people all moving in unison like line dancers at a Western hoe-down. The roots of Tai Chi come from within. I can still see Al on the deck in the late fall sunlight, inviting each of us to tap into that inner life

2.7 TAI CHI

force and let the force move our bodies in tune with our world. That was pure meditation!

The body's life force, vital energy, the Chi (Chi in China, Ki in Japan) is already within you. It flows naturally. Tap into it. Release it. And when inner Chi moves in harmony with the Tao—the energy everywhere in nature and in the universe—then you are one with everything!

Understanding the Tao, Chi and Tai Chi are actually very simple. Nothing metaphysical, or mysterious, or esoteric, or new age. Simple to grasp. Words and books are unnecessary, just a knowing smile. It is. You just flow with it.

Of course if you're serious about a regular practice, a good teacher like Al Huang can make it fun teaching you such details as "grasping the bird's tail and repulsing the monkey." But most of all a good teacher can help you take the TaoSports approach into your entire fitness and athletics program and on into the business world and your everyday life.

And being with others who are also practicing Tai Chi lets you share your Chi energy in a synergistic social environment, while enjoying a meditation the Taoists call "Circulation of the Golden Light."

DISCOVERING "THE TAO OF INNER FITNESS"

In *Working Out, Working Within,* Huang and Lynch distinguish the prevailing attitude of modern sports from TaoSports in an effort to enhance our performance not just in athletics, but in our business and personal lives:

"Traditionally, athletics and fitness are battlegrounds for war against an opponent, a clock, scoring goals and other external concerns. The Tao of Inner Fitness, on the other hand, views sports as an arena for the battles within, where your obedience to athletics and fitness cannot be separated from the search for life's verities."

And although this is a Chinese Tai Chi master and an American sports psychologist speaking, their message is remarkably similar to what we hear from stress management clinicians and neuroscientists testing monks:

THE SPORTS/FITNESS ZONE

"Physical life gives our spiritual path a boost as we stare in the face our inner concerns of fear, fatigue, failure, patience, perseverance, courage, confidence, ego, self-doubt and a host of others that affect our growth as athletes and people. What we notice is the way that sport and exercise can transport us to a new level of awareness beyond the game itself, to a place where all our external successes and accomplishments are the mere reflections of the victories within against these demons. We not only have the opportunity to become better athletes, we can become better people as well."

THE PRINCIPLES OF THE TAO ARE ALIVE IN EVERY SPORT!

It is difficult to convey in a few paragraphs the essence of Tai Chi and TaoSports, as well as the Tao itself which has been so eloquently described in the 2,500 year old Taoist classic, the *Tao Te Ching*. And yet, this context is essential in order to truly understand Tai Chi. Here is a summary of the eight qualities of The Tao from *Working Out, Working Within:*

1. **Spontaneity**: Tze Jan—Being your authentic, spontaneous self.
2. **Noninterference**: Wu Wei—Live your life cooperating and flowing in harmony with nature and its seasons rather than fighting against it.
3. **Stillness in Motion/Movement in Stillness**: Tai ji—Balanced and centered within, you expand your inner power by exercising externally.
4. **Polarity balancing**: Yin Yang—Tao sees and balances opposites in one concept, integrating the Yang-assertiveness with Yin-receptivity.
5. **Change and transformation**: I Pien—Accept and move in harmony with the cycles and seasons of nature, the rhythms of your own being.
6. **The Vital Force of Life**: Yung Qi—Everything, everyone around you has Chi, meditate on it, tap into it, get into action and expand your power.

2.7 TAI CHI

7. **Personal Power**: Te—envelope your inner strength through actions, in the real world, facing life's challenges, positively, doing the right thing.
8. **Windflow Grace**: Feng Liu—The Tao flows gracefully and naturally like the wind and the water. Flow with it, enjoy being one with it.

This exploration into Tai Chi here turned out to be a nostalgic journey back into my days as an Esalen work scholar where I entered the world of my Tai Chi master, Chungliang Al Huang. He showed me his way of life for a few brief moments in time on a warm sunny weekend at Esalen in the late fall overlooking the blue Pacific.

THE MASTER TRANSFERS HIS POWER

He was just Al Huang to us, a real nice guy. Only later did I realize how great teacher we had walking with us, someone who in simple words and movements, communicated 2,500 years of the Tao, wrapping it in Tai Chi and his new world of Tao-Sports.

The night Al Huang left Esalen I had a dream unlike any other in my life. We were together in China, in his world, long ago before the great revolution. We were trying to escape the enemy. I had lost my Marine Corps I.D. cards. Al was going to cut off his hands and give them to me, to help me escape. Deep mythic symbolism, said my therapist later.

This Tai Chi master wanted me to take his hands, his energy, his Chi, to help me go beyond my "China," go where there are no masters, to create my own identity, become my own teacher, and pass on this gift. That is the message of all great masters. Be the real you, go on a journey of self-discovery.

Al was passing on his power as he had done for so many others. And I got it. I was in a midlife crisis, in a transition near the end of a long journey through the rigid logical authoritarian world of the Wall Street and Corporate America, once again in uncharted territory, set free.

THE SPORTS/FITNESS ZONE

SWIMMING & SURFING
AS MEDITATION

*The path of surfing, presents similarities
with the paths of all people who have sought meaning
and found their essence, whether through surfing,
practicing za-zen, or studying the Tao.*
Jean-Etienne Poirier
Dancing The Wave

*Surfing is the simple act of walking on water.
There are many other ways to ride an ocean wave
... but when we say 'surfing,'
we really mean walking on water,
or at least standing on it.
This is what makes surfing unique,
we walk on water.*
Drew Kampion
The Way of The Surfer

THE AWARENESS THAT water sports are a natural way of meditating came to me while sitting in a Soho loft in New York City back in the mid-seventies, far from the great waves off the coasts of California, Hawaii and Australia. An advertising executive friend insisted I go with him to a Joseph Campbell workshop in Soho. At the time I knew nothing about Campbell, but with a name like *Mythical Meditation*, the workshop sparked my imagination.

At first his ideas about meditation seemed all over the map, literally, ranging far and wide throughout history and around the world. Campbell saw meditation in everything from Jungian

2.8 SWIMMING & SURFING

psychology, Zen Buddhism, Taoism and Christian mysticism, to Hopi shamanism, the Tarot, astrology, and the paranormal. And yet ... by the end of the workshop, Campbell had not only changed the meaning of meditation for me, he literally changed my life.

SWIMMING LAPS—MEDITATING ON THE TAROT

At one point near the end, when someone finally asked him how he meditated, Campbell, a competition swimmer in his younger days, combined the mundane and the mysical by explaining that he meditated on the Tarot cards while swimming laps in his backyard pool, combining his morning physical exercise with this meditation.

Actually, swimming and all water sports offer a natural way to meditate, thanks to the essential need to control the breathing. On one hand, consider all those poor young monks sitting in a cold Zen temple somewhere in Japan, struggling endlessly to focus on their breath in their early meditation exercises.

BREATH-CONTROL
NATURAL MEDITATION FOR ALL SWIMMERS

The average swimmer, however, has no choice about whether to learn the discipline of breathing. None! "Breath control is an essential ingredient in all swimming," says David Thomas in *Swimming: Steps to Success,* "recreational swimmers, speed swimmers, synchronized swimmers all need to learn correct breathing habits."

Of all the water sports, however, surfing goes beyond pure meditation. For the million men and women surfers worldwide, surfing is a spiritual path, their way of searching for the meaning of life, of their essence, of nature, of the divine in the mysterious gandeure of the great waves.

Watch them: Surfers are indeed "walking on water" in fact and in spirit. The surfer at once embraces and transcends everything Thich Nhat Hanh, the great Buddhist master and meditation teacher, wrote in *Living Buddha, Living Christ:* "Our true home is the present moment. The miracle is not to walk on water, the miracle is to walk on the green earth in the present moment."

THE SPORTS/FITNESS ZONE

"WALKING ON WATER"
IN SEARCH OF THE PERFECT WAVE

Surfers are both the miracle and the "not-miracle:" Balancing on the board they are very much in the present moment, they are walking on water and they walk on the green earth too, at least the green earth inland beyond the sandy beaches. Here's how surfer Gerry Lopez, nicknamed 'Mr. Pipeline' and the 'Buddha in the Barrel' put it:

"Surfing requires you to deal with the Here and Now more intimately than any other thing I know. Life in general tends to lead people away from the present, making them deal with the past and future (recollection and anticipation) much more than is healthy. Surfing is a spiritually uplifting endeavor, but it takes a long time before you discover that ... I think you just keep getting reborn until you figure out that enlightenment is an attainable experience."

Lopez has that rare impish grin of a high-priest, a native kahuna or a Zen master who, if he hasn't actually ascended into nirvana yet, he sure is having a whole lot of fun along the way. Lopez is a surfer's surfer, one of the early adventurers who rode the unrideable waves beyond the outer reefs of Maui.

"RIDING THE WAVE"
THE PATH TO ENLIGHTENMENT & NIRVANA

Today the "Buddha of the Barrel" is in the business of building boards and inspiring the next generation: "Life is just like surf. It comes up, it goes down, but there's always something happening. Perhaps the greatest lesson of surfing is the gift of spontaneous reaction—flowing with it on a wave is much easier than flowing with it back up on the beach. It certainly helps you to move around things that seem to stop a lot of people."

There are over a million surfers in the world today, most live and work in the everyday world, waiting to the right moment to escape into their special watery nirvana. The surfers I know, including a pro football quarterback and a house painter, are like all surfers, very independent people who are quite secretive and protective of their private inner world.

2.8 SWIMMING & SURFING

SURFING IS NOT SOMETHING I DO
IT IS WHO I AM

In *The Way of the Surfer,* Drew Kampion eloquently captures the surfer's "Zen mind. Everything is waves. This was the vision of Albert Einstein. It is the lesson and the truth that emerges, over time, out of the surfing experience. Surfing is a natural act, but complex natural act. To ride the wave is to explore the universe of balance—balance within balance within balance. Without balance, a ride cannot be sustained. Without balance, a wave cannot be sustained. Without balance, nothing can be sustained. It sounds like the ancient wisdom of Lao-Tzu in the Tao Te Ching."

Enter their world for even a brief moment and you sense that surfers have some secret that belongs to them alone, a secret that can only be passed on in private by a Zen-surfing monk who has been there, done that, and then only to dedicated disciples who will guard it and not reveal the secret to just anyone.

Their secret is that surfing is the miracle of "walking on water" and surfers are living the miracle. Ask them, they will tell you: "Surfing is not just something I do, *it is who I am."* And in being totally who they are, they live in one of the world's most natural meditations, at one with the universe, and on a path to enlightenment and nirvana here on earth—*every time they "walk on water!"*

THE SPORTS/FITNESS ZONE

FLY FISHING
AS MEDITATION

*In our family, there was no clear line
between religion and fly fishing, We lived at
the junction of great trout rivers in western Montana,
and our father was a Presbyterian minister and
a fly fisherman who tied his own flies and taught others.
He told us about Christ's disciples being fishermen,
and we were left to assume, as my brother and I did,
that all first-class fishermen on the
Sea of Galilee were fly fishermen
and that John, the favorite,
was a dry-fly fisherman.*
Norman Maclean

SO BEGINS NORMAN Maclean's haunting classic, *A River Runs Through It.* You don't have to live in western Montana, or have a minister for a father, or tie your own flies to know that somehow fly fishing and God and meditation all go together.

In fact, talk at length to any fisherman and you know that deep down fishing really is an intensely personal spiritual experience whether they're fly fishing for trout in Montana, deep sea fishing for marlin off the coast of Florida, casting for tonight's supper off a California piers, or quietly trawling holes canoeing the still lakes of Ontario, Canada, where I spent one summer.

2.9 FLY FISHING

GREAT "FISH STORIES" ARE DEEP WITH SPIRITUAL TRUTHS

Listen closely and you'll hear more than one "fish stories"—*some macho bragging about the size of the catch, endless details about the one that got away, or some amusing anecdotes about strange happening out there on the water*—stories that fishermen know normal people will accept so they aren't left with the simple impression that the whole day was spent swatting bugs and slogging all the way upstream through the woods hauling all that gear—just to catch that little fish?

The truth is, fishing is a unique way of meditation that normal people will *never* really understand. Fishermen get something out there on the water that they never really get sitting in church, although they may not admit it to their pastor. And yet, most won't go so far as to label it a spiritual experience—or even meditation—because all that's something best left to monks sitting around in monasteries, not average folks in trout streams.

But what they do get fly fishing out there on the running waters is a little peace of mind and a break from the so-called real world, the kind of serenity Thoreau discovered at his Walden Pond retreat.

"I say *inner* peace of mind," says another Montanan, with the emphasis on *inner,* which is really where meditation begins and ends anyway. It's just something you feel inside you that's hard to share, hard put in words, and intensely personal, especially since you know it really does have everything to do with God—you just don't want to come across as preachy or arrogant.

SITTING MEDITATION TAKES ON NEW MEANING IN THE RIVER WATERS

Maybe calling fly fishing meditation, or spiritual, really is just too personal, too mushy, exposing your soul too much, or just too difficult to put into words … or maybe it's just a way to hold it in your special private world.

And yet there are others like Maclean who give voice to this way of meditating: "I've sometimes thought this inner peace of mind, this quietness is similar to if not identical with the sort of

THE SPORTS/FITNESS ZONE

calm you sometimes get when you go fishing, which accounts for the popularity of this sport," said Robert Pirsig in, of all places, *Zen and the Art of Motorcycle Maintenance.*

"Just to sit with the line in the water, not moving, not really thinking about anything, not really caring about anything either, seems to draw out the inner tensions and frustrations that have prevented you from solving problems you couldn't solve before and introduced ugliness and clumsiness into your actions and thoughts."

HALL-OF-FAMER MEDITATES ON FISHING IN LOCKER ROOM BEFORE FOOTBALL GAME!

We hear a similar reverence in Peter Kaminsky's *The Fly Fisherman's Guide to The Meaning of Life:* "The fly rod is the tool I use in my pursuit of happiness, and a very particular kind of happiness it is. When I have the fly rod in my hand and water all around me, time stops ... I enter a different reality ... it is just you and the world, moving in sync ... it makes me feel whole."

Rams defensive star and Hall-of-Fame great Merlin Olsen and golf legend Jack Nicklaus were both lifelong fly fishermen, both often making the day trip down the famous Green River in Utah. In fact, Olsen regularly calmed his nerves before a football game—by visualizing fly fishing, in the Rams locker room!

Meditation? You bet! These unique experiences are what meditation is all about when it's at its best—contentment, feeling whole, and finding a little peace of mind out there. It's about focusing on the silence, enjoying the beauty of nature surrounding you, letting go and just flowing with what's happening in the world. And in your better moments, communing with your creator, just you and the fish, out there on the river.

PILGRIMAGES TO EXOTIC FISHING SANCTUARIES

Yes, fishing is meditation at its best, and knowing that brings a warm smile across my mind as I think about how much all those poor monks are missing as they sit for hours cross-legged in their cold drab monastic cells. Makes me want to whisper in their ears: "Get up, sneak out, you'll find the peace you're searching for out

2.9 FLY FISHING

there, out on the running waters, where the fish are the greatest of teachers—as they once were long ago on the Sea of Galilee."

And with that smile comes the urge to send some adventurous monks Chris Santella's exotic *Fifty Places to Fly Fish Before You Die,* a book guaranteed to entice them on a new kind of spiritual pilgrimage—searching for nirvana with rod'n'reel in such far-flung places as Mongolia, Zambia, Chile, Norway and South America.

True, Santella admits he's only fished about one third of these heavenly sanctuaries. But somehow, there's so much of his soul lingering on each page of this beautiful travel adventure book that you somehow know that someday, over his life-time, Santella's love of fly fishing will eventually carry him to all fifty of the world's exotic fly fishing destinations. Although most fishermen just keep going back to familiar holes and streams, where the spirit comes alive again.

A RIVER RUNS THROUGH IT
"I AM HAUNTED BY WATERS"

You sense this is true because for people like Maclean, Kaminsky and Santella, fishing and life are the same thing—a wondrous journey with a river running through it. The journey is beautifully captured in the haunting final paragraphs of Maclean's masterpiece, where late in life memories overlap and fly fishing remains the one line that makes each man's life essential to the entire universe:

"Like many fly fishermen in western Montana where the summer days are almost Arctic in length, I often do not start fishing until the cool of the evening. Then in the Arctic half-light of the canyon, all existence fades to a being with my soul and memories and the sounds of the Big Blackfoot River and a four-count rhythm and the hope that fish will rise.

"Eventually, all things merge into one, and a river runs through it. The river was cut by the world's great flood and runs over rocks from the basement of time. On some of the rocks are timeless raindrops. Under the rocks are the words, and some of the words are theirs.

"I am haunted by waters."

THE SPORTS/FITNESS ZONE

GARDENING & DAILY LIVING
AS MEDITATION

Meditate on foods ...
I'll take a piece of really
good chocolate and I'll spend five minutes eating it.
If you pay attention to what you're eating,
you don't eat as much of it.
Dean Ornish, M.D.

At 8:30, sleep. Most important meditation!
Sleep is the common meditation
for everyone, even for birds.
The most important meditation.
Not for nirvana, but for survival.
Dalai Lama.

When you are hungry, eat.
When tired, sleep.
Zen wisdom

YES, I KNOW, you think this one doesn't belong in "sports-fitness." That it may not even be meditation? That's why it's here! To keep you stretching your ideas about meditation further. Eastern masters encourage us to live with a "beginner's mind"—open to seeing things fresh. Westerners call it "thinking outside the box." So try this one for size: If anything can be meditation, then perhaps anything can also become a sport, athletic activity and fitness routine.

3.0 GARDENING & DAILY LIVING

POLICE COMMANDER MEDITATES IN HIS GARDEN

Gardening comes under this heading. A Los Angeles police commander once told me he got more out of being in his garden than going to church on Sunday. If you want to feel this spirit more, read Woods and Glover's *Gardens for the Soul,* Ashmun and Mandell's *Garden Retreats,* Julie Messervy's *The Inward Garden,* or Elizabeth Murray's delightful little book *Cultivating Sacred Space, Gardening for the Soul.* They all remind me of my sabbatical working on the Esalen farm in the Big Sur—meditating all day with nature.

Murray says "gardening can be a joyous and mindful form of meditation as you sow the seeds of relaxation and watch your pleasures grow." Such a description of gardening may not fit the macho sport image, especially for a police commander. But then, both yoga and tai chi were long considered light-weight feminine sports by men in America, until recent years. So think outside the box, keep an open mind in what you "see" as a sport and as meditation.

BLIND NINJA IN ANCIENT SAMURAI WARGAME

Here's another unusual meditation that demanded my total focus. While at Esalen I participated in George Leonard's "Samurai Game" with fifty other people from around the world. Leonard is an Aikido master and author of *The Ultimate Athlete* and *Mastery: The Keys to Success & Long-Term Fulfillment.*

We were divided into two medieval Samurai armies commanded by warring shoguns. The rules were arbitrary, controlled by the gods (a role played well by Leonard's darkside!). The battle went on for hours, with successive duels between us Samurai. After being killed, I miraculously reincarnated as a blind, one-armed Ninja ... and fought the final winning duel!

Sport? Meditation? Yes, if you think outside the box, once you truly know that anything you do, *anything,* can become a meditation—*if you focus solely on what you are doing, and nothing else.*

In *Mastery,* Leonard says "every Zen master will tell you that building a stone wall or washing dishes is essentially no different from meditation. The quality of a Zen student's practice is defined as much by how he or she sweeps the courtyard as by how he or she sits in meditation."

ALL OF LIFE IS A MEDITATION
JUST DO WHAT'S IN FRONT OF YOU

Remember The Karate Kid film? A teenager begs a retired martial arts master to teach him how to fight. The old master reluctantly agrees, then hands the kid a bucket of paint and a brush with simple instructions: Paint the fence around the house! The kid's disappointed, but starts painting begrudgingly. At the end of the day he's exhausted, shows the master he finished the job.

Not done, the master tells him, more to paint! Start again tomorrow. Days go by with the kid doing endless, meaningless tasks until he's totally frustrated, tells the master he's had it! Good, now his training moves to a new level where he learns that all of those boring tasks were the basic skills he needed as a fighter.

"All life is a meditation, most of it unintentional," said Joseph Campbell responding to a question from Bill Moyers in *The Power of Myth*. Life teaches us many lessons while we think something else is going on. And only later do we learn the value of what we learned, often by doing mundane, everyday chores reluctantly, either as unintentional or intentional meditations. The choice is yours.

SCIENCE & ENGINEERING AS MEDITATION

"Making coffee, brushing our teeth, driving the freeway, changing the baby's diapers, the list of everyday opportunities for practice is endless and joyous, as long as we don't make some distinction between sacred and profane activities" says Misha Merrill in the introduction to *Zen at Work: A Zen Teacher's 30-Year Journey in Corporate America.*

The author of *Zen at Work,* Les Kaye, was an IBM design engineer before retiring. His work was his meditation, much in the same way that Alan Watts discusses the Japanese physicist, Dr. Kunihiko Hashida in *The Way of Zen:* "Every human activity can become a form of za-zen meditation ... Hashida, a lifelong student of

3.0 GARDENING & DAILY LIVING

Zen and the editor of the works of Dogen, never used formal za-zen. His Zen practice was his study of physics."

TEMPLE MONKS RAKE STONE GARDEN
THERAPIST RAKES RUG AT HOME

In his work, *Care of The Soul,* Thomas Moore also tells us that "The ordinary arts we practice every day at home are of more importance to the soul than their simplicity might suggest."

My wife taught me the truth behind Moore's subtle insights. She is a psychotherapist with a full schedule. We had a cleaning woman, and yet many days she would slowly and quietly go around the house dusting, watering plants, raking the rug. I finally realized that these were her ways of meditating, as profound as a monk raking the stone garden in a Buddhist temple.

"Work, usually manual labor, is traditionally an important part of Zen practice," say Blackstone & Josipovic in *Zen For Beginners.* "People living in monasteries clean the buildings, cultivate the grounds and wash an inordinate number of dishes as part of their daily activity."

NO WORK, NO MEDITATION, NO EAT

The stress of daily life was in many ways no less intense in ancient times than now—why else their relentless focus on meditation as a way to peace! The authors note that "the man credited with establishing 'work practice' in the Zen schedule is Po-chang Huai-hai, an 8th century Zen master who coined the phrase, 'a day without work is a day without food.' ... When he had grown quite old, his students became worried that he would make himself sick by working so much and contrived to hide his garden tools. No problem, the old master simply stopped eating until his tools were returned to him."

Similarly, the Swiss psychologist Carl Jung considered his retreat on Lake Bollingen essential to peace of mind: "Talking is a torment to me, and I need many days of silence to recover from the futility of words. Without my piece of earth, my life's work would not come into being ... I have done without electricity, and tend the fireplace and stove myself. Evenings, I light the old lamps. There is no running water, and I pump the water from the well. I chop the wood and cook the food. These simple acts make man simple; and how difficult it is to be simple."

COOKING'S GOOD FOR THE SOUL
CHOCOLATE'S GREAT FOR THE HEART

Every simple chore becomes an opportunity for meditation, something spiritual masters understand for centuries in both Western and Eastern cultures. They understood the simplicity in doing whatever work is in front of you at this moment: Of not "confusing spirituality with 'thinking' about God while you're peeling potatoes—you just peel the potatoes."

The 17th century French monk Brother Lawrence found his spirit as the monastery's cook: *"The time of business does not with me differ from the time of prayer, and in the noise and clatter of my kitchen, while several persons are at the same time calling for different things, I possess God in as great a tranquility as if I were upon my knees at the blessed sacrament."*

The cook has also been one of the most revered positions in the ancient and contemporary Buddhist meditation practice, as we see evident in such delightful books as Kimberly Snow's *In Buddha's Kitchen* and the classic, *Instructions to the Cook,* co-authored by Bernard Glassman, an aeronautical engineer who is now a Buddhist teacher and an entrepreneur who founded Greystone Family Inn, a homeless shelter, and other non-profit organizations.

Opportunities for meditation exist all around us, every moment throughout the day. Eating is perhaps the most obvious one. We read in Deepak Chopra's *Chopra Center Cookbook:* "Always eat with awareness, gratitude, respect and delight."

And America's foremost heart specialist, Dr. Dean Ornish, meditates while slowly eating and enjoying a small piece of chocolate, something I also discovered while losing forty-eight pounds on the WeightWatchers plan.

3.0 GARDENING & DAILY LIVING

WHEN TIRED AT THE END OF BUSY DAY
DALAI LAMA SAYS "SLEEP IS BEST MEDITATION"

And at the end of a good day's work and meditating on the utter simplicity of that most ancient of all Zen sayings, "When hungry eat, when tired sleep," rest assured that you are in the best of company, for His Holiness, the Dalai Lama says: "At 8:30, sleep. Most important meditation! Sleep is the common meditation for everyone, even for birds. The most important meditation. Not for nirvana, but for survival."

Remember, anything can be a meditation—the choice is totally up to you!

THE CREATIVITY ZONE
10 ways to meditate with passion & enjoy life!

3.1 — **CREATIVE VISUALIZATION**

3.2 — **PERSONAL JOURNALS**

3.3 — **CREATIVE WRITING**

3.4 — **THE MUSICAL ARTS**

3.5 — **DANCE MEDITATION**

3.6 — **ACTING & PERFORMING ARTS**

3.7 — **PAINTING & THE FINE ARTS**

3.8 — **CRAFTS & HOBBIES**

3.9 — **AN ARTIST'S DATE**

4.0 — **THE ART OF "DOING NOTHING"**

THE CREATIVITY ZONE
OF MEDITATION

*Leap, and the net will appear.
God has lots of money. God has lots of movie ideas,
novel ideas, poems, songs, paintings, acting jobs.
God has a supply of loves, friends, houses that are
all available to us. By listening to the creator within,
we are led to our right path.
On that path we find friends, lovers,
money, and meaningful work.*
Julie Cameron,
The Artist's Way

ONE OF THE great things about this new way of meditation is that you can meditate while you continue doing things you already love doing, where your way of meditating is effortless, making what you already love doing even more enjoyable; moreover, you probably won't think of it as "meditation."

Seriously, it is so easy and natural to slip impreceptably into this creative zone of meditation and not even know it—as if you are guided by some mysterious force. Then suddenly, you're in it, filled with a sense of peace. One of my favorite mystics, Veronique Vienne, captures it this way: "You are enlightened, though you don't know what it means ... let alone care about it." It just is and you just are. All creative meditations have this mysterious quality.

THE CREATIVITY ZONE

GO INTO THE CREATIVE ZONE AND MEDITATION WILL HAPPEN NATURALLY

Without "thinking" about it, a paradoxical sense of peace and passion envelopes you when you enter this zone. Somehow—*you're not really sure how*—it all just happens naturally, without "thinking" about it you are creating, and meditating, and you feel complete. That's the best kind of meditation.

You can increase the odds of this happening. How? Easy. First, select experiences that you already know make you feel good without working at them! That's right, make whatever you're doing into a meditation. Stuff that's fun, enjoyable, pleasurable. Let me repeat that for emphasis: *Pick something you love doing anyway, and then, let it become your way of meditating!*

In fact, anything you love doing creatively will work. Creativity is pure meditation, and creative activities—*singing, playing a musical instrument, painting, photography, sculpture, knitting, dancing, journal writing, acting, hobbies of all kinds, and all other creative activities*—are natural ways everyone uses to meditate.

And yet most people don't think of the creativity activities they're doing as 'meditation'—they're just enjoying what they're doing! We've got this strange belief that meditation has to be difficult. Or we feel guilty because we're escaping from being productive. Or because somewhere in the past we were told that having fun can't possibly be meditation, because meditation is something you work at and struggle with.

Fortunately many others know that creative expression arises naturally from a spirit deep within us that cannot be denied. Perhaps that's why so many creative people describe what they're doing in spiritual terms, with a profound sense that they have been given a gift from the gods, something to be embraced with passion and with a sense of gratitude toward some mysterious, universal creator.

YOU BECOME ONE
WITH YOUR INNER CREATOR

The creative zone is the place most people naturally go to meditate. In fact, we all go there quite often, not as professional artists to make

THE CREATIVITY ZONE

a living, we go there because the urge to create is in every living being, without exception.

So as you read through these creative ways of meditating, stop for a few moments every now and then. Ask yourself how often you escape from the stresses of everyday life and slip naturally into a meditative state by tapping into the creative power within you, each in some small way—*it may begin as innocent and simple as humming in the shower, admiring a work of art in a gallery, writing a little poem on a card to your mother, making a special dinner for loved ones, reading a novel, patiently listening to a small child read a fairytale to you, or even designing the cover of a business report.*

Creative meditation is a state of mind and spirit that emerges naturally from deep within you, joyfully and without much effort on your part, it just happens. Trust it, for in these meditations you are tapping into a powerful inner creative spirit.

Remember the Four Simple Rules of All Meditations

Rule One
Focus on what you're doing this moment—*and nothing else*

Rule Two
Anything you're doing can become a meditation—*anything*

Rule Three
Trust yourself, the results are within you—*discover your way*

Rule Four
Keep it real simple, everybody meditates—*we do it naturally*

THE CREATIVITY ZONE

CREATIVE VISUALIZATION
AS MEDITATION

*Visualization is an active form of meditation
in which you relax and chose to view
images in your minds eye that will
influence your emotions and energy.
Visualization is a natural process.
It lets you tap into your inner sources of
peace and calm so you can
respond positively to events in your life.
What you see in your mind's eye can strongly
influence your beliefs and achievements.
Chungliang Al Huang & Jerry Lynch
Thinking Body, Dancing Mind*

ACTUALLY THERE ARE two kinds of visualization: The first one is the more traditional, passive visualization most of us naturally begin with. The second is an action-oriented visualization which is essential if you want results in sports or the tough, competitive business world. You should be using both of these powerful meditation tools—in fact, you already are and don't realize it.

The passive one comes from Shakti Gawain's *Creative Visualization*: "Creative visualization is the technique of using your imagination to create what you want in your life. There is nothing at all new, strange, or unusual about creative visualization. You are already using it every day, every minute in fact. It is your natural power of imagination, that basis creative energy of the universe which *you use constantly, whether you are aware of it or not.*"

3.1 CREATIVE VISUALIZATION

CREATE THE LIFE YOU WANT
IN FOUR SIMPLE STEPS

Gawain's four basic steps for an effective creative visualization are so simple anyone would agree that we are indeed already using this method of meditating "every day, every minute in fact." It can't get any simpler than these four steps: One, set your goal. Two, create a clear picture. Three. Focus on it often. And four, give it positive energy, using frequent mental reinforcement with affirmations. This kind of visualization is a passive, mental activity.

ACTION-ORIENTED VISUALIZATIONS

Using "positive thinking" visualizations by themselves—for example, the universally popular "every day in every way my life is getting better and better"—will reinforce your resolve to achieve goals. But taken alone, they are still passive mental exercises. To ignite the full power of this meditation technique, you have to get into action, as most of us learn over time.

So at the other end of the spectrum, you'll find the *action-oriented* visualization. We have already seen that sports psychologists, athletic coaches and fitness trainers use this meditation technique all the time in training the physical body.

In fact, today the process of visualizing a golfer's swing, a skater's creative program, or a gymnast's routine—*of mentally rehearsing before the action*—is as normal a part of the pre-training process as the physical training, working out with weights, going cardio and stretching.

ACTIONS SPEAK LOUDER THAN AFFIRMATIONS
IN THE BUSINESS WORLD

However, unlike the sports world, in business arena physical action is all too often not the natural goal of the office environment—*sitting at a desk and thinking is!* So there is the strong possibility your visualizations may never get translated into action plans.

You sense this potential problem in a revealing comment made by Chuck Norris in *The Secret Power Within*. Norris worries that people may use Eastern meditation practices to justify a passive approach in business, by fostering a belief that passive meditation makes it okay to sit, meditate and visualize, with the expectation that some external force will make your dreams come true.

GET INTO ACTION & TO THE BOTTOM LINE!

That's a misreading of the Eastern mind: "Although many people don't realize it," says Norris, a successful businessman, "Zen is not about monks meditating as much as it is about *taking action,* making decisive moves in the present. There's a certain impatience about Zen, an unwillingness to get lost in meandering arguments, a desire to cut quickly to the essential, or to *get to the bottom line."*

Yes, get to the bottom line! At one point in his life Norris had forgotten this key principle. Some years after he retired as a world champion martial artist and was a successful businessman, he lost his sense of direction, "had no goals." During dinner one night, his friend Steve McQueen suggested he take up acting. But months later he told McQueen he had "serious doubts" about becoming an actor.

VISUALIZATION TRIGGERS A WAKE-UP CALL

McQueen looked at Norris in disbelief: "Remember that philosophy of yours that you always stressed to students: *Set goals, visualize the results of those goals, and then be determined to succeed by overcoming any obstacles in the way.* You've been preaching this to me for two years, and now you're saying there's something you can't do?"

That was his wake up call—an epiphany, enlightenment, brain storm! Norris realized that when it comes to business decision making, you better put visualization in a stronger context, as part of a bigger package—yes, you do set goals, yes, you *visualize the results* you want, but then you must get into action and make it happen. Visualization must go beyond wishful thinking. Get to the bottom line, where visualization is a very action-oriented form of meditation.

3.1 CREATIVE VISUALIZATION

CREATIVE VISION—ONE OF THE 7 HABITS OF HIGHLY EFFECTIVE PEOPLE

Creative visualization is also what other business leaders call "vision!" Management guru Stephen Covey, author of *The 7 Habits of Highly Effective People* and *First Things First*, tells us: "The power of vision is incredible ... Vision is the best manifestation of creative imagination and the primary motivation of human action. It's the ability to see beyond our present reality, to create, to invent what does not yet exist, to become what we not yet are. It gives us the capacity to live out of our imagination instead of our memory."

For many people like Covey, creative visualization is not merely an ego-driven way to satisfy purely personal and material needs, but energy coming from higher source. Covey is quite clear in this regard: "Spirituality cannot be something a person toys with, a little compartment of our lives. It has to be at the core, in a way that affects every other part of our lives."

Similarly, Gawain tells us that knowing that your creative visualization, your vision, is coming from "source" makes it ever more powerful, where "Source means the supply of infinite love, wisdom, and energy in the universe. For you, source may mean God, or the universal mind, or the oneness of all, or your true essence. However we conceptualize it, it can be found here and now within each of us, in our inner being."

THE SOURCE OF ALL CREATIVE VISION "THIS THING CALLED YOU"

In fact, the single most powerful expression of this connection between creativity, visualization and spirituality comes from a little book of meditations that has sustained me much of my life. In *This Thing Called You*, Dr. Ernest Holmes, founder of the Science of Mind, urges us to recognize and honor our creative visualizations as coming from another source:

"The desire you have to be something, to do something, is a mental echo in your mind of the Spirit which already exists within you. It is an impact of your divine and spiritual self upon your mental or psychological self. It is the Spirit in you seeking an avenue of expression through you. It is the real Self you would like to be, the deep spiritual Self having all knowledge, having access to all power, being one with Life. This is the Self that can heal the sick and raise the dead. It is the transcendent, triumphant self."

Once you tap into this higher source, this thing called you—*and get into action*—whatever your mind can visualize, *it will create.*

"THE CREATIVE MIND" OF A WINNER

One of the most powerful—*and fastest*—examples I know on how you can tap into the power of creative visualization comes from Cy Young award winning pitcher Barry Zito of the Oakland Athletics. Back in 2001 he was in his second season with a losing 6-7 record and a lackluster 5.07 earned-run average. His dad, a classically-trained musician who conducted for Nat King Cole, sensed the problem and came to Barry with one of Ernest Holmes' books, written in 1918:

"He introduced me to *Creative Mind* and he stayed with me" for four days leading up to Barry's next pitching start. They read *Creative Mind* for five to seven hours a day, recorded tapes and put up signs around his room "affirming who I was, and the power I have." Barry finished 17-8 and lowered his ERA to 3.49. Now that's one powerful visualization!

PERSONAL JOURNALS
AS MEDITATION

Why should we write?
We write because it is human nature to write.
Writing claims our world
It makes it directly and specifically our own.
We should write because humans are spiritual beings and
writing is a powerful form of prayer and meditation,
connecting us to our own insights and to
a higher and deeper level of inner guidance as well.
Julia Cameron

JOURNAL WRITING IS a popular meditation tool because it focuses people naturally—and it works. We all have a story to tell, although for many it is personal and private and often untold. And yet, it is who we are—*our life, our soul, our story, and it longs to be told, even if just to yourself.* It is expressed in many ways, some will verbalize the story, some express the message in their actions and behavior, many others feel compelled to put the words on paper.

In high school I keep diaries. Later, letters, albums and memoirs when I was with the Marines and traveling in Asia. And throughout my adult life, volumes of journals. Writing seemed easy, until I spent eight hours struggling with my first college English paper, a one-page three-hundred word epic that earned a "D" grade.

INNER VOICES DEMANDING TO BE FREE

But criticism never stopped me. Yes, it hurts, but in the end you get over it, it's just one more obstacle in life to overcome. You find out why. Then you do it better next time out of the blocks. Remember: We all have a story to tell. And it will come out. That's why journal writing is so natural for meditation.

Demons and gods, little boy and little girl voices all demand release from deep in our heart and soul. And in my case, an overload of childhood memories about drunken, angry parents who suffered their own demons, memories that still haunt me, and to this day still find their way into my journals.

As a result, most of my life I've had to live with regular bouts of acute anxiety and panic attacks, although I didn't talk much about them and hide them well. Today I realize that for many others like me, writing is a release valve, an escape pod, a safe haven from these memories. If you and I sat down, I know your story, like mine, would also have a storehouse of haunting memories that all too frequently emerge unpredictably and uncontrollably from deep within to overwhelm the rational façade we present to the world.

Call it meditation, prayer, therapy, journalizing. Call it whatever you like, within each of us there is a secret story that wants told. It has a mind and a drive of its own. As science fiction master Ray Bradbury put it in *Zen and the Art of Writing,* "I do not write. The *other me* demands emergence constantly … to tell me who I am behind this mask. He the Phantom is, and I façade."

For some, journal writing is painful because the secrets are so dark and the risk of exposure so frightening that resistance seems impossible to overcome. For others it is an escape from reality, a comforting sanctuary, a welcomed relief. And a rich mixture of both for so many of us.

YES, YOU CAN OVERDOSE ON MEDITATION

There was one ten-year period when I was newly recovering from years of self-destructive alcoholism, where I would sit obsessively and write in my journals, often for hours on end, exploring all the incredible insights triggered during therapy sessions and self-help program inventories. I was also working sixty-hour weeks on Wall Street, writing reports and professional articles, and on evenings and weekends writing screenplays and a musical comedy.

3.2 PERSONAL JOURNALS

Finally, I felt so trapped in this obsession to escape into the comfortable safe territory of my journals that I had a friend toss a bankers box filled with ten years of my journals into a dumpster—in an undisclosed location—so I that wouldn't change my mind and go retrieve it.

Did that dumpster dump set me free? Yes. Temporarily. Did it *stop* me? No. "The truth is that writing cannot be given up," says Julia Cameron. You may get angry, even hate it, but never for very long. Whether professional or amateur, "it" will quietly come clawing back to the surface. In the past couple decades the "other me," as Bradbury calls it, has written eight books and over three million words as a journalist ... *and another twenty volumes of journals!*

SO WHY DO IT ... BECAUSE IT WORKS!

For most of my life, journal writing has been a natural way of meditating for me. It works. And it obviously works for millions of others. Julia Cameron is unquestionably the world's leading guru on the subject, thanks to her classic, *The Artist's Way,* the recognized bible of journal-writing meditation. She says "Morning Pages," as she call them, "are my way of meditating, I do them because they work." Get it? Journal writing works as meditation!

And they "are not intended for writers only ... they work for anyone, for painters, for sculptors, for poets, for actors, for lawyers, for housewives, for anyone who wants to try anything creative ... Lawyers who use them swear they make them more effective in court. Dancers claim their balance improves, and not just emotionally."

Thankfully, journal meditation is very simple to do. Too simple for most traditional meditation gurus. There are no secret rituals or special format, no mantras or chants, no breathing exercises, no unusual diagnoses, no cryptic terms, and no detailed steps to follow. In fact, meditation gurus marvel at the utter simplicity of this one:

"The tool I ask you to undertake now is the most profound writer's tool I have devised or experienced," says Cameron. "This tool is the bedrock of a writing life. Morning Pages bear witness to our lives. They increase our conscious contact with spiritual guidance." They are "*a potent form of meditation for hyperactive Westerners.* They amplify what spiritual seekers call 'the still small voice'."

THE PERFECT WAY ANYONE CAN MEDITATE
KEEPING JOURNALS ABOUT DAILY LIFE

It's so easy to do: "Morning Pages are three pages of daily longhand, strictly stream of consciousness. They are about anything and everything that crosses your mind. They may be petty, whiny, boring, angry. They may be cheerful, illuminating, insightful, and introspective. There is no wrong way to do them." Just write three pages!

When I first read *The Artist's Way* back in the mid-nineties I thought: How wonderful, I have been meditating this way naturally for over twenty years. I knew they worked because I had long-term proof of what she meant: "It is impossible to write morning pages for any extended period of time without coming into contact with an unexpected inner power."

That's exactly what I found using this journal meditation tool: "Higher forces speak to us through writing. Call them Inspiration, Muses, Angels, God, Hunches, Intuition, Guidance, or simply a good story—whatever you call them, they connect us to something larger than ourselves that allows us to live with greater vigor and optimism."

You don't even have to wait until tomorrow morning—right now, write now, write three pages or one or ten. Trust the process. Let the magic unfold. Tell your story to yourself, this is the one natural way each of us meditates.

CREATIVE WRITING
AS MEDITATION

*For us the preparation of this book
has itself been a meditation.
It has been permeated from the outset
with the love and spiritual purpose that
we have come to know and treasure
through our guru, Nem Karoli Baba.
We offer it to you as
an invitation to join the feast.
Ram Das and friends
Journey of Awakening:
A Meditator's Handbook*

EVERYONE HAS A book in them, a story that wants to be told. Most of us keep it inside, hidden in a corner of our soul, or shared as anecdotes among family and friends. Many use personal journals as an ongoing dialogue with ourselves, as a private way of meditating.

There is a very thin line between writing personal journals in our private chambers and becoming a published writer, cross that thin line and suddenly all your writing is meditation.

In fact, writing is such a perfect way to meditate, you feel drawn to it all day, every day! And even when this way of meditating is not easy or peaceful, not church-like spiritual, even when it is an endlessly frustrating struggle, even then it is the perfect opportunity for meditation.

THE CREATIVITY ZONE

ATTITUDE OF GRATITUDE—POSTITS ON MONITOR

There are little postits all around the edges of my monitor. Daily reminders of this incredible experience as a working writer, making a living at it. I know I've been given a wonderful gift.

And yet often in the daily struggle that comes with this gift, I forget, and I need these reminders to be grateful. So, little notes keep going back and forth between me and some mysterious creator. The current note just above the center of the keyboard reads:

> *Writing this book is your conscious contact with the creator within you. Expect miracles. Focus, trust and The Creator will show you the best way.*

And yet I could kick myself for waiting so long—it took me almost fifty years to cross that thin line from journal writing to being a working professional.

As long as I remember I've wanted to write: Diaries in high school. Later a campus newspaper columnist. My articles appeared in a couple hundred professional journals over a few decades, self-promotional and marketing stuff that many business and financial executives write, not to make a living, but to build name recognition in the business world.

"AH-HA!!"

Then at age fifty-seven came the ah-ha moment, an epiphany, a sudden awareness that what I loved most in life was writing. Regardless of which career I was in—banking, law, film, architecture, real estate, psychology—writing was my true love. I knew then that I had no choice. I had to become a full-time writer, which meant making a living at it. I had to "do what I love, and trust the money would indeed follow!"

Easier said than done. That fear kept me, and keeps many others, on the safe side of the thin line. The first four years were scary—like most other writers, I was tested. Made little money. Loaded credit cards going deep in debt. But I had to do it: Edited a financial newsletter. Self-published a book. Finally got three successive books published by a major house. I was still struggling when "the break" finally came, an unexpected fluke. I was offered steady work as a financial journalist during the dot.com boom. More books got published. I was finally making a living as a full-time professional writer.

GET LOST IN THE CREATIVE PROCESS AND BECOME ONE WITH THE SOURCE

Finally, after six years I became aware of how powerful writing is as a way of meditating. One day was especially intense and busy. I got lost in writing all day. Suddenly I noticed it was dark out. Everyone had left, hours earlier. I finished what I was doing, shut down the computer, made copies of some drafts to review later at home, grabbed my coat and briefcase, locked the door and turned to walk toward the elevator.

We had a long gray, nondescript hallway that snaked around to the elevator bank ... then something struck me ... I broke into a smile ... a sense of peace came over me ... I really was doing what I love ... and yet, I got so lost in what I was writing all day I never once thought about God, as I occasionally do ... nor thought that the day was some kind of spiritual experience ... nor that it had been the perfect meditation ... *and yet it was all that and more!*

Then as I began "thinking" about the day, a new "story" began emerging ... whoever God was, he, she or it must have been thinking about me all day, even if I wasn't thinking about them ... and that this day was exactly what meditation and spiritual experiences were all about, without ever thinking about it that way ... and *that* got a real good chuckle ... suddenly I was aware that all that happened really didn't need an elaborate post-mortem, with fancy labels ... yet there I was, labeling it! So I went home, had dinner with my wife, a good laugh, and got totally into some mindless television program.

Maybe that day would have been as equally memorable a spiritual experience if I had been in any other business or profession, I sure hope so because I want the same for everyone. But I am certain it happened to me while writing. And I know that a life of writing is my way of meditating, it is my conscious contact with my inner creator and the Creator of the Universe!

THE CREATIVITY ZONE

RELEASING DEMONS ... AND CREATIVE GODS!

The great masters echo the same message. Take the prolific science fiction writer Ray Bradbury, author of the classic *Fahrenheit 451*. In *Zen and the Art of Writing: Releasing the Creative Genius Within You*, Bradbury teases us: "What, you ask, does writing teach us?"

> *First and foremost, it reminds us that we are alive and that it is a gift and a privilege, not a right. We must earn life once it has been rewarded ...*
>
> *Second, writing is survival. Any art, any good work, of course, is that. Not to write, for many of us, is to die ... I have learned, on my journeys, that if I let a day go by without writing, I grow uneasy. Two days and I am in tremor. Three and I suspect lunacy ... An hour's writing is tonic ...*
>
> *We use the grand and beautiful facts of existence in order to put up with the horrors that afflict us directly in our families and friends, or through the newspapers and TV ...*
>
> *The poets and artists of other years, long past, knew all and everything I have said here ...*

How about you—uneasy? Near lunacy? Afraid you won't survive? Don't feel alive? *Write, write, write!* This is one meditation that works with or without knowing why. Just write, in writing you will release the demons, and release the creative genius within you, for you will be in contact with some mysterious universal creator that wants out. And as Bradbury says, releasing both of them is the fire that makes for great books.

3.4 THE MUSICAL ARTS

THE MUSICAL ARTS
AS MEDITATION

Music is meditation,
if it is sung soulfully by good singers,
or even if it is sung badly by singers with soulful hearts ...
Music is the inner or universal language of God.
I do not speak French or German or Italian,
but if music is played from any of those countries,
immediately the heart of the music enters into my heart,
or my heart enters into the music.
At that time no outer communication is needed;
the inner communion of the heart is enough.
My heart is communing with the heart of the music,
and in our communion we become inseparably one.
Meditation and music cannot be separated.
Sri Chinmoy
Indian spiritual master

MUSIC IS PERHAPS the purest of all natural meditations—everything from songwriting, composing melodies, playing our favorite instruments, singing a solo ballad, enjoying gospel singers at a local church, a string quartet, rock opera, or a concert hall filled with the sounds of a large choir and orchestra. And for every performer, there are thousands enjoying their music.

A MUSICAL MEDITATION WHILE COMMUTING

Music has always been one of my favorite meditations: Often while on a three-month sabbatical at Esalen I'd drive into Carmel. This

THE CREATIVITY ZONE

hour-long stretch of the Big Sur coastal road is one of the world's most dramatic. The twists and turns force you to stay on high alert. And yet, after making the trip several times the route seemed programmed in my system. With the Phantom of the Opera music as a backdrop I would slip into a trance-like meditation—and become one with the gentle winding road, the music, nature and the universe.

Years later Norman Fischer, a Zen abbot and poet described this kind of meditation: "I'm in my car, on the highway. I turn off the news and the baseball game I've been listening to and switch to a Beethoven violin sonata that's loaded in the CD player. Listening to the music, my mind gradually starts to release, like a hand that had been grasping something tightly and is beginning to let go. Another mind appears, a mind completely engaged with the pattern the music weaves. A moment before I had been frozen into the shape of a self in a world. Now, the music has thawed me out."

MEDITATE ANYTIME, ANYWHERE, ANY MUSIC

What a perfect way to meditate—whether you're just one in an audience of thousands at a huge rock concert, or listening with head phones on a treadmill in the gym. Music naturally resonates within the human mind, lifting the emotions, the spirit and the soul, music is meditation in its highest form. Anything musical is a perfect meditation:

> —You could be singing a favorite song in the shower, whistling on the way walking to work, sitting and humming on a park-bench during lunch, all great times to meditation for a moment anytime during the day.
>
> —As a performer, meditating while singing a solo ballad or playing the harp at a wedding, in a band, quartet, choir, chamber ensemble, a large orchestra—or in the audience, listening, focusing on the sounds.
>
> —Musicians meditate playing the cello, flute, tuba, piano, guitar, drums, saxophone, zither, xylophone—

3.4 THE MUSICAL ARTS

any musical instrument, even a ticking metronome, is an instrument for meditation.

—Any musical form can become a meditation: Rap, rock, jazz, soul, R&B, Latin, opera, Kabuki, bluegrass, show tunes, barbershop quartets, cabarets, piano bars, lullabies, holiday carols, karaoke and ballroom dance music. Whatever your passion, go with it, trust it, let it become your way of meditation, naturally.

—Lyrical Gregorian chants, guttural Tibetan chants, Aboriginal, African and Native American shamanic ritual chants, or the haunting sounds of whales, loons, seashores and thunder storms, every one offering an opportunity to connect with nature at a primal level.

—You may resonate with the sounds of Motown, Nashville, New Orleans or Harlem—meditate on your culture, your heroes and heroines, your dreams, discover the creative spirit and be lifted by its music.

Music is a way of meditating for non-musicians as I discovered back in the mid-eighties. I went to a workshop at the Esalen Institute in the Big Sur just because the name was so unusual: "Music for Non-Musicians."

Thirty of us were given sticks and bottles, bells and noisemakers of all kinds, even a few real musical instruments like sousaphones, harmonicas, a violin and some horns, although few knew how to play any of them!

We were definitely non-musicians, "musically-challenged" you might say, and yet we played a hauntingly beautiful music! We played from the heart, from somewhere deep in the soul—you could sense it in our solos, the quartets, even as a full orchestra. Our "music" was created spontaneously in the moment, we had to focus, trust and flow because we were truly in alien territory. Besides it was so darn energizing we just didn't want to miss a beat.

THE CREATIVITY ZONE

THE UNIVERSAL LANGUAGE OF THE SOUL

When the delightfully inventive musical "Stomp" came along a few years later, I was reminded of my non-musician's experience. Stomp used far out noise-makers, like garbage pail lids, large trash cans, brooms, matchbooks, and anything handy in a musical production which the producers said has no words, and yet:

"Everyone can understand it. It has little or no melody in the traditional sense, so it doesn't matter if your taste in music is jazz, classical, dance or pop. Stomp is about rhythm, which is common to all cultures. Everyone knows rhythm, if only from the beating of their own heart—it is the basis of all music."

The *Los Angeles Times* added: Stomp "reminds us that art can be made anywhere out of anything." The overlap here is obvious, making art, making music and meditation can be created anywhere ... anytime ... out of anything ... and simultaneously. Remember, meditation is very simple, "all you need to do is focus on one thing, what you are doing," says Philip Toshio Sudo in *Zen Guitar*.

BEATLES MUSIC WAS A SPIRITUAL ADVENTURE

Music is already part of the harmony of the universe. It's everywhere in nature and throughout the world. Listen. Feel it. Make music your meditation by connecting your spirit with the universal music.

The Beatles are a classic example, they were meditating quite naturally through their music and in their lives every day, when playing simple love songs about adolescent love, like "I Want To Hold Your Hand." And other times when the message was more deeply metaphysical in "Tomorrow Never Knows," where Lennon uses the Tibetan Book of the Dead.

And yet, it's not the content that makes a song meditation, neither of those songs is necessarily better for meditation. *The only thing that matters is the experience of the meditator, not the music.* The Beatles music was so successful because their music was their meditation:

> —**George Harrison** spent his life searching the spirit world: "Everything else can wait but the search for

3.4 THE MUSICAL ARTS

God cannot ... It doesn't matter if you're the greatest guitar player in the world, if you're not enlightened, forget it ... I'm really quite simple, I don't want to be in the business full-time because I'm a gardener. I plant flowers and watch them grow."

—In one of his poems **Paul McCartney** asked, "God where are you?" and the answer came back, "I am here in every song you sing." When asked about his all-time hit "Yesterday," he said: "It's amazing to me that it just came through me. That's why I don't profess to know anything; I think music is all very mystical ... Well, you're dead lucky if something like that passes through you."

—When the Beatles returned from a trip to India to study and meditate with guru Maharishi, they came back disappointed. In fact, **John Lennon** wrote a satirical song about the guru and another song about a friend traveling with them who went into meditation overload: "She'd been trying to reach God quicker than anyone in the Maharishi's camp: who was going to get cosmic first? *What I didn't know was I was already cosmic."*

The truth is, the Beatles didn't need to go to India, music was their meditation. Lennon finally realized he was already in that spirit. Harrison knew all along, and never stopped searching. And McCartney not only spoke with God, he even got a reply. They were the messengers—and the message!

CANCEL THAT TRIP TO INDIA, JOURNEY WITHIN

They went off to India because like most of us, they had doubts, they wanted assurances, and at the time they weren't aware that their music was their path to enlightenment—always had been.

Would the Beatles have chosen Tai Chi as their meditation if they had gone to China? Or perhaps taken up surfing, golf or tennis as an alternative way to meditate if they had lived in California instead of

England? Maybe. But what we do know is they had already found what they were looking for back home, every day, in every song, in every session, in every performance. It was there all along for them and for everyone in their audience.

In the final analysis, meditation comes from within the meditator, not from some guru out there, nor in a distant land, nor locked in some secret mantra. Meditation is within the musician, it is the music of the heart and the soul, and *each one of us has a musician within us.*

MUSICAL MEDITATIONS TO "BLOW YOUR MIND!"

Music is such a powerful meditation tool because it naturally taps into all of our senses and emotions, into our heart and soul at a deep level—music is so successful and efficient as meditation simply because it naturally bypasses our thinking mind, giving it a chance to rest and enjoy some *peace of mind,* or more accurately, "peace *from* mind," while it heals and renews our soul.

This way should be obvious. However, it is not because most executives are trapped in their thinking brain for hours every workday, often at maximum overload. As a result, the rational brain is not the best meditation channel, nor are sitting meditations. In fact, the mental zone and sitting meditation will likely *increase* your stress because they force your thinking mind to confront itself with itself. Music, on the other hand, is an alternative route bypassing the thinking mind, it is the perfect way to get you "out of your head."

When your mind shifts into a music channel—either as a creative artist or a music lover—you know you are one with the music, that you are meditating, you know something inside you is in touch with the universal spirit, you know you have gone into a place where you can hear a still small voice say to you, as it said to McCartney: "I am here in every song you sing," and in every musical number you will ever hear—*so meditate on that!*

3.5 DANCE

DANCE
AS MEDITATION

O' humans, learn to dance!
Otherwise the angels in Heaven will not
know what to do with you.
St. Augustine

Dance is one of the most beautiful things
that can happen to a man.
So don't think about meditation separately.
Meditation is needed as something separate
for people who don't have any deep creative energy;
no direction for their energy to get
so deeply involved that they can be lost.
But a dancer, a painter, a sculptor,
need not have any other meditation.
Rajneesh
The Orange Book:
Meditation Techniques

FIVE YEARS ATTENDING a dance meditation class in New York's Soho district convinced me that *dance is meditation.* Dance is one of the most natural forms of meditation in the world. Go with the music and you become the dance, whether solo or with a partner. A dance meditation can happen anytime—even if you are just watching the Joffrey Ballet, Salsa dancers, or Sufi dervishes in St. John the Divine's Cathedral during Christmas celebrations.

THE CREATIVITY ZONE

You can lose yourself in the Tango, Polka or line dancing. You enter another world without ever leaving this one. You become the dance. And it can be as subtle as a mental rehearsal, visualizing each move of a new dance, imperceptibly rocking to music silently playing in your mind. Dance blends body, mind and spirit in a flowing motion—because dance is meditation.

DISCOVER THE "DANCER WITHIN" YOU

My work in dance meditation started during a group therapy exercise. Our psychologist asked us to stand, silently, eyes closed. After several minutes he asked us to think of the one word that described our essence. When we had it, we were to say it softly to ourselves, gradually louder. Mine was "dancer."

"Dancer!?" Me, a totally rational Wall Street investment banker. Me, a *dancer?* Where the heck did that come from? Today I know, it was from some mysterious creative force hidden deep inside searching for a way out. That force is in all of us. In you too. Mine was "dancer," what's yours?

Not long afterwards, I met Calvin Holt in a prison. Calvin was a Hatha Yoga teacher and the flamboyant owner of Manhattan's chic Serendipity III Restaurant. Calvin was attending a play put on by inmates and directed by his girlfriend. A friend asked me to go with him.

During an intermission, Calvin invited me to a weekly dance meditation group in his Soho loft. Little did I know what I was getting into, but the inner voice from my therapy group suddenly seemed like a hot clue in a scavander hunt.

DANCE MEDITATION TRANSFORMS BANKER

Over the next five years I rarely missed a session in spite of a demanding schedule. On one long business trip for a bank client I flew back from San Antonio after a midday meeting. A limo picked me up at LaGuardia, took me to Calvin's loft for the class, and waited. Afterwards I went back to the airport for the red-eye and caught up with our Morgan Stanley team in time for meetings in

3.5 DANCE

Albuquerque the next day. In many ways, that dance meditation was with me throughout the trip, it had become who I was, a "dancer."

Our dance sessions were improvizational, in a huge loft bordering Little Italy, lit only by candles. Occasionally Calvin spoke softly in what seemed like a lost ancient language, revealing simple lessons of life in movement, blending the natural and the supernatural. He was the Tao, he was a Zen master.

Actually I wasn't so much listening to his words as sensing his energy, drawing from his wisdom, and growing stronger for it against background music from many eclectic sources—lyrical Gregorian chanting, soothing sounds of the sea, modern jazz, harsh guttural Tibetan chanting—and always ending the evening on a high note with the haunting Pachelbel's Kanon.

Although unconscious of it at the time, in retrospect it's now obvious that those years in Calvin's weekly Soho dance meditation class complimented everything else going on in my personal growth—every one of my acting classes, therapy sessions and self-help meetings that were slowly freeing me from Wall Street's rigid left-brain mindset.

THE DANCER BECOMES THE DANCE
MEDITATION IN MOTION, LOST IN THE MOMENT

Dance meditation was not a stepping stone to becoming a professional dancer. That's not why we were doing it. For some it was great exercise. Others did it because it was lots of fun. Also a kind of self-help therapy. And a chance to socialize with other creative spirits, while freeing yours. More likely, a little of each.

Professional dancers venture far beyond, they are the fortunate ones—for them dance is life, they have an opportunity to become the dance and to live in a world vibrating with dance meditation, all day, every day. You sense it in the many imaging techniques of choreographer and dance teacher Eric Franklin in his *Conditioning for Dance: Training for Peak Performance:*

"Conditioning the dancer as an athlete and as an artist is a mind-body exercise—strength, balance, flexibility, alignment and imagery training need to come together as a balance whole," says Franklin. "Mental presence and concentration are the solid foundation of mind-body training. *Being present in movement* means experiencing the moment-to-moment changes in the shape and dynamics of every part of the body."

If you listen closely you sense he could be coaching a marathoner, consulting with an inventor, training a martial artist, or instructing a monk. *The message is the same in every case.* As these activities become your meditation—the dancer becomes the dance, the inventor one with process of inventing, the runner is the race, the martial artist merges with his opponent. Remember, you are meditating when you are *totally engaged in doing whatever you are doing in the moment—and nothing else.*

THE SILENT LANGUAGE OF THE SOUL

The next time you do a little dancing, anywhere, try making it your meditation—whether you're in a ballroom with the love of your life, attending a wedding or New Year's celebration, line dancing at a western barn dance, enjoying disco on a Saturday night, salsa, tap, rap, teaching a child their first dance steps, or skipping along the sidewalk from the restaurant back to work!

Carry with you the message of the great Martha Graham: "Dance is the hidden language of the soul." At first it may be faint, as in my therapist's office. But listen, for it is there—whispering, waiting. Let the words come as movement for "you are unique, and if that is not fulfilled," says Graham, "then something has been lost." Become the dancer. Make your life the dance. All day, every day, for *dancing is meditation.*

3.6 ACTING & THE PERFORMING ARTS

ACTING & THE PERFORMING ARTS
AS MEDITATION

*We meditate to discover our identity,
our rightful place in the scheme of the universe.
Through meditation,
we acquire and eventually acknowledge
our connection to an inner power source
that has the ability to transform our outer world.
In other words, meditation gives us not only
the light of insight but also
the power for expansive change.*
Julie Cameron
The Artist's Way

YES, ACTING IS one of the more unconventional ways you can meditate. And yet, for many of us in the business world, it offers a perfect opportunity for personal growth. Remember, anything can be meditation. You are already a performer—*the star in your life story.* You have every reason to become the best "actor" you can possibly be.

Seriously, if you want to become a top performer in business, take acting lessons for a while. You'll probably find out, as I did while studying acting and directing in New York City, that acting lessons offer a rare combination of creative expression, personal therapy and meditation, as well as a great way to prepare yourself for business presentations, negotiations, sales meetings, financings, and lots more—all from this one creative activity!

THE CREATIVITY ZONE

In fact, everyone in business should study acting for a while. Even if you never appear on Broadway or even in your local community theater, you will improve your chances of success in business, sharpen your edge as a creative thinker, and enjoy a more balanced, peaceful life.

"ALL THE WORLD'S A STAGE!" ESPECIALLY THE BUSINESS WORLD

Admit it, if you're in business today, you're always on stage, always performing, you always have an audience—bosses, employees, customers, bankers, investors. If you want to succeed, you better be an actor, and a good one at that, whether you like it or not.

You have no choice, it doesn't matter where you're working, in Corporate America, on Wall Street, or as an entrepreneur, you are putting on a show. *You are acting all day, every day*—selling, communicating, on the phone and in person, maybe a new project, explaining production schedules to your staff, rolling out a new marketing program, talking with employees, schmoozing clients at lunch, pitching them over drinks, appearing on camera, public testimony, dealing with lawyers, bankers and suppliers, delivering speeches to professional societies and civic organizations.

A GOOD ACTOR IS NOT "ACTING"

You are always on stage, always putting on a show, always a performer. And if you truly want to succeed on that stage, you have to become a good actor. But does that mean you must become *more* of a phony, *more* "the act," *more* identified with the role you're playing?

Quite the opposite. It means getting more into the real you, more in touch with what really makes you tick on the inside, so that the outsides—the actor and the performer—are more authentic and genuine. It means connecting the act and the real you, not losing yourself in the act. It means making absolutely sure that every day you and the actor are one and the same, no split personality.

Lee Strasberg, the great Method Acting teacher said performers should "try *not to act* but to be themselves," simply speak and gesture as they would normally. However, that's not an easy task for an actor

3.6 ACTING & THE PERFORMING ARTS

in a theater or in a business setting, because we want to impress your audience.

ACTING UNBLOCKS YOUR POWER

This is scary stuff, because you're in a double-bind—damned if you do, damned if you don't. If you *don't* become a better "actor," you'll probably never reach peak performance in business or in life. But if you *do* try to become a better actor, you'll have to dig deep into your soul and expose who you really are, and that's too scary for most people.

Either way it's a tough journey because the stuff inside us makes us freeze with stage fright and performance anxiety. We all have secrets that block us. They prevent us from tapping into our full potential. They hold us back from becoming a top performer in business and a truly great actor in the drama of life. Acting wasn't easy, but it was one of the best things I ever did—a great meditation, supportive therapy during my midlife transition, and it opened me to changing careers.

STRASBERG'S 'METHOD ACTING' AS MEDITATION

While working on Wall Street with Morgan Stanley I took lessons at a couple acting schools in The Village: First the Sonia Moore Theater Academy. Moore wrote *The Stanislavski System: Professional Training of an Actor.* Then later I studied at The Strasberg Theater Institute, where "method acting" originated. Both are based on the work of Constantin Stanislavski, a Russian acting teacher who is regarded as the father of modern acting.

In *An Actor's Handbook,* Stanislavski describes several tools used by the great actors, tools which are surprisingly similar the traditional meditation methods used in today's mind-body and stress management clinics. Acting coaches rarely use the word "meditation" when explaining their acting techniques, but the similarity between the two is unmistakable in three of Stanislavski's examples:

> **Focusing without distractions**—"Concentration of attention…creativeness is first of all the complete concentration of the entire nature of the actor …

THE CREATIVITY ZONE

In watching the acting of the great artists ... their creative inspiration is always bound up with their concentration of attention."

Creative visualization—"The creative process starts with the imagination ... We can use our inner eye to see all sorts of visual images ... every invention of the actor's imagination must be worked out."

Relaxation response—"Relaxation of muscles ... at time of great stress it is especially necessary to achieve a complete freedom of the muscles. In fact, in the high moments of a part the tendency to relax should become more normal than the tendency to contract."

Although the choice of terms are different, Stanislavski and modern acting coaches use many of the same tools and work toward the same goals as sports psychologists, mind/body clinicians, stress management experts, motivational speakers, media coaches and others who understand the benefits of meditation in their respective professions.

ACTING LESSONS—DOORWAY TO NEW CAREER!

Acting was great for me—although I never went professional, taking lessons paved the way to a new career path as I shifted out of a dominant left-brain, logical personality into the freer right-brain creative world! Your path will be different but probably no less unpredictable than mine:

Acting lessons with Sonia Moore, then later at The Strasberg Institute were followed by an audition at an off-off Broadway theater that resulted in an offer to act in an Eugene Ionesco play, a *Hell of a Mess*

During this period I also wrote a script for a horror film, after that, a thriller about a financial takeover involving the mafia, and then a musical comedy based on *Goethe's Faust*

3.6 ACTING & THE PERFORMING ARTS

> I had a great time with some acting monologues from Chekhov's *Cherry Orchard* and Richard Brook's filmscript, *Marat/Sade*
>
> I joined a TV Academy Workshop for wannabe directors, writers and actors where I directed a short film, *Ophelia's Mascara* that later won a Gold Medal at the Virgin Islands International Film Festival
>
> That got me a fellowship at the American Film Institute as a student-producer, which got me out of Morgan Stanley and New York City
>
> Eventually I wound up in the Hollywood scene at the Financial News Network where I was executive vice president of almost one thousand hours of live television news
>
> Later I became executive vice president of Michael Phillips film company, Mercury Entertainment Corporation when it went public. Michael was also producer of *The Sting, Close Encounters of the Third Kind* and *Taxi Driver.*

All this happened over a ten year period. My friend Dan Travanti, Captain Furillo in The Hill Street Blues television series, once put all of life's twists'n'turns into perspective: "You have to run like hell to left field. Then magically you end up in right field. You don't know how that happened. But if you aren't running out to left field, you never get to right field."

ACTING, MEDITATION & THE MIDLIFE CRISIS

Acting is a great way to meditate, maybe not for everyone, but it certainly was for me. And I know there are many other left-brain, super-rational folks in the business and financial world going through a seemingly endless mid-life crisis asking, "is that all there is?" questioning their career path.

All the work I was doing in the performing arts complimented everything else I was doing in personal development and recovery;

seeing a therapist, attending self-help meetings and going to a dance meditation group. All part of the searching people do in the business world, quietly, behind the scenes.

This may also be part of your journey. Remember, I was working at that venerable old House of Morgan when all this started quite by accident. Maybe you're working somewhere in Corporate America or on Wall Street, maybe you're curious—what have you got to lose? Besides, you don't have to give up your day job or even tell your friends at the office. Explore. Take the risk. As Julie Cameron says in *The Artist's Way,* "Leap and the net will appear."

TAKE A COURSE IN "ACTING FOR NON-ACTORS!"

If there is a little voice nudging you to risk something new, here's a simple suggestion. Go online and search for courses in "Acting for Non-Actors." When I checked, over 250 entries came up, including one in New York City at the Learning Annex. Another at the Self-Expression Center in Houston explained the course in a delightfully inviting way:

Acting for Non-Actors: Discover the Thrill of Acting. Ever thought you could act? Thought acting would increase your self-confidence? You are right! Acting is not about faking or pretending. It's about being genuine in the moment. Acting for Non-Actors will help you discover you can act. You will work with short scripts from plays and movies. Simple step-by-step techniques will help you relax and feel confident on stage and in daily life. Learn how to:

- Free yourself to be real on stage and in life.
- Develop the presence of a star.
- Create rapport with others.
- Listen and respond spontaneously.
- Activate your creativity.

Go ahead, listen to that little voice inside you. Find one of these courses on "Acting for Non-Actors" near you. Think outside the box, push the envelope, take the big risk, and venture out beyond your comfort zone! You'll never regret it.

3.6 ACTING & THE PERFORMING ARTS

Remember, you're already an "actor" in the business world, every day. You're on stage performing all day for one audience after another.

So why not learn how to become a better actor, sharpen your creative talents in the process while improving your opportunities for success in the business world, and maybe even find a new career, add some balance and peace to your life, meet new people, and have some fun too!

Acting, performing, what a beautiful way to meditate. Try it, you have nothing to lose and everything to gain—*discover the real you!*

Leap, and the net will appear.

THE CREATIVITY ZONE

PAINTING & THE FINE ARTS
AS MEDITATION

Many of us wish we were more creative.
Many of us sense we are more creative,
but unable to effectively tap that creativity.
Our dreams elude us. Our lives feel somehow flat.
Often, we have great ideas, wonderful dreams,
but we are unable to actualize them for ourselves.
Sometimes we have specific creative longings
we would love to fulfill—playing a piano,
painting, taking an acting class, or writing.
Sometimes our goals are more diffuse.
We hunger for what might be called
creative living—an expanded sense of creativity
in our business lives, in sharing with our children,
our spouse, our friends.
Julie Cameron
The Artist's Way

FEW BUSINESS AND financial executives are as adventurous as Paul Gauguin who traded his position in the Paris banking world for a new life painting in the peaceful island of Tahiti. Most of us stay behind, stuck, afraid, rationalizing, struggling to find some balance, while our creative needs all too often get squeezed into infrequent and brief breaks from the stresses of today's hectic business world.

Some people, fortunately, do find this balance of "creative living" while actively engaged in the real world. While on Wall Street with Morgan Stanley mine were acting, dance and writing. Here are some other examples.

3.7 PAINTING & THE FINE ARTS

JUNG & CHURCHILL—A WINDOW INTO THE SOUL

The Swiss psychologist Dr. Carl Jung's painted an unusual series mandalas over many years. One publisher tried to convince him that "the fantasies arising from my unconscious had some artistic value and should be considered art." He decided to keep them private, a window into his soul: "At first I could only dimly understand them, but they seemed highly significant, and I guarded them like precious pearls" as he explored his inner self.

Winston Churchill took a less analytical approach: "I paint only for enjoyment" he wrote in his book, *Painting as a Pastime;* "We cannot aspire to masterpieces. We may content ourselves with a joy ride in a paint-box." What started "as a lark" became his "constant companion" for over forty years. And very personal, the first public exhibit of his paintings opened late in his life, in France, under an assumed name.

A pastime yes, and an opportunity to meditate. For anyone with a creative right-brain that's brimming with ideas, sitting silently with your eyes closed is likely to take no more than a few seconds, as a way of meditating on what you want to see appear on the canvass—before launching into the action!

A painter will also be meditating as brushes swirl, as paints are mixed, as pencils are sharpened. Isn't that what meditation is all about: Focusing solely on what you are doing ... on whatever you're doing in the moment ... and only what you are doing? It can take you through an afternoon painting England's sea coast, as Churchill often did. Or as simple as a moment doodling during a boring business meeting, or sketching birds in a local park after a lunch break.

YOU FIND PEACE-OF-MIND IN THE DOING

"A sketch can take five minutes or an hour; it can be full of detail or sparse in line," says Dr. Patricia Monaghan and Eleanor Viereck, "Neither time nor appearance are important in using natural sketching as a meditation. What is important is the process: focused looking, combined with hand motions that activate the right side of the brain, lead to a sense of calm, well-being, and peace."

In fact, as kids we were all more in touch with this inner artist, until the "real world" distracted us. I would often lose sense of all time sitting for hours in my grandparents' attic, sketching the presidents, painting pictures of birds or working on some art poster for the prom or other school event. Later I found an outlet in the field of architecture, today I still search my inner world for clues about the meaning of life, sketching as I write in my personal journals.

IN SEARCH OF THE "ARTIST WITHIN"

The inner and outer worlds of the professional artists come together in their work, for they know full well that what they are doing is "an outward expression of an inner life in the artist," as Edward Hopper put it in one of his reflective moods describing what happens to him on a psychological and spiritual level while painting.

Other artists feel it more as a spontaneous, sensory explosion of passion as some inner creative force takes over your body and mind and forces its way to the surface: "I can't do anything but paint, the paintings just come to me," says Jackson Pollock.

"When I am painting I am not aware of what I am doing, because the painting has a life of its own."Similarly, Picasso said; "A painting is not the result of working toward a goal, it is a stroke of luck, an experience." Much the same as it was for Churchill.

The word meditation doesn't quite capture the experience of the creative artist, but it comes close! Art is their life, all day, every day. Meditation is an inactive process for monks and new age gurus sitting silently doing nothing. On the other hand, the creative spirit in the artist demands action, something deep within needs to be set free, needs to get what's in the soul onto canvas and paper, clay, stone and steel—and in that process their art is a meditation much like the moving meditations of the Chinese Taoists in Tai Chi and calligraphy.

DISCOVER "THE REAL YOU" IN YOUR ART

Today there are artists worldwide who teach "Art as Meditation" courses for anyone who might, "on a lark," want some guidance in reconnecting with the inner artist that we all knew so well as

3.7 PAINTING & THE FINE ARTS

children. For example, Di Skelly Heron, an Australian artist, invites people to her "Art as Meditation" program with these wonderfully warm promises:

1. Learn to re-connect with your creative spirit through the medium of painting and to interpret your paintings.
2. Understand your relationship to colors and how to use them as a way to communicate with your intuitive self.
3. Learn how to create an ongoing dialogue with your inner self through painting journals.
4. Break through the 'intellect versus the imagination' barrier and paint from your heart not your head.
5. Relax and have fun.

Now that should bring a smile to the face of your inner creative self!

UNIVERSITY "ART-AS-MEDITATION" PROGRAMS

Closer to home you'll find an extensive "Art-as-Meditation" program at Matthew Fox's University of Creation Spirituality in Oakland, California. Fox is a priest and a visionary theologian. His program integrates "the wisdom of western spirituality and global indigenous cultures with the emerging scientific understanding of the universe and the passionate creativity of art."

The Art-as-Meditation curriculum of the University of Creation Spirituality has a course on "Painting as Meditation" integrated with other creative, psychological and spiritual experiences: Tai Chi and yoga, drumming and dance, mask-making, chakras and dream work, and journeys in Native American and African rituals. Their curriculum makes this way of meditating an adventure that will satisfy anyone's creative urges.

MEDITATION IS "A JOY RIDE IN A PAINT BOX"

"Creativity is an experience, a spiritual experience," says Julia Cameron in her classic *The Artist's Way*. In the mind of the painter, the sculptor, and other artists, creativity, spirituality and meditation are not separate things, they are one and the same. "It does not matter which way you think of it: creativity leading to spirituality or spirituality leading to creativity. In fact, I do not make a distinction between the two."

So it is impossible to distinguish them—*between creation, spirituality and meditation*—for the process of creating art is spirituality in action and a perfectly natural way to meditate. Winston Churchill would quickly dismiss all the fancy talk about spirituality, creation and meditation. My guess is he'd tell us to just let your creative child have a little fun and take "a joy ride in a paint-box."

3.8 HOBBIES & CRAFTS

HOBBIES & CRAFTS
AS MEDITATION

> *Meditation ought to decrease the drivenness*
> *of our lives, not make it worse.*
> *That is why I say meditate for its own sake,*
> *as a hobby ... don't become an expert,*
> *but stay a beginner's mind.*
> *Like a hobby, meditation ought to be*
> *a time when you can occupy your mind*
> *with something for its own sake,*
> *without getting caught up in any of*
> *your usual occupations.*
> *Clark Strand*
> *The Wooden Bowl*

HOBBIES ARE ACTIVITIES you love to do for relaxation, things outside your everyday occupation, like woodworking, knitting, model making, photography. Things you're passionate about. Sometimes they evolve into a business. Most the time, hobbies are a little money and a lot of enjoyment.

And that's why a hobby is a perfect opportunity to meditate, a natural way to meditate, and you don't even have to call whatever you're doing meditation. I love the way Clark Strand, a former Buddhist monk, puts it in *The Wooden Bowl:* Meditation should be "like a hobby." When it feels like a job, the idea of meditation disappears. Better to see it as an escape from the stresses of the everyday business world.

THE CREATIVITY ZONE

YES, HAVE FUN! THIS MEDITATION IS ABOUT DOING WHAT YOU MOST ENJOY DOING

This is the easy path, the high road. By using your favorite hobby as your meditation, you're able to do something you already know you love doing, you get to concentrate totally on it, without distractions, and you can enjoy the moment, every moment, naturally. Best of all, it won't take you any extra time.

You just do it whenever, and as long as you feel like it. And it doesn't take any extra time: So you don't have to worry about finding 20 minutes in the morning (time away from your kids and reading the newspaper) and 20 minutes in the evening (time from your spouse and your favorite television shows) to do sitting meditation.

That way, everything meditation promises—time away from the stresses of the business world, relaxation, balance and a feeling of peace—are all there as part of your favorite hobby, and that's your meditation.

Most traditional systems of meditation take themselves far too seriously. That's not really what it's all about. Meditation is about liberation, not confinement. As Strand writes in *The Wooden Bowl:* "Once meditation rises above the level of play, its possibilities are diminished. Why? Because when meditation loses its lightness it becomes like everything else—an object of desire. When we meditate for something other than meditating, we only become further ensnared in the endless cycle of getting and spending, whereby every activity has to have a goal."

Hobbies are the perfect way to meditate for the pure pleasure of doing what you're doing. In fact, with your favorite hobby you don't even have to force yourself to focus and concentrate. When a hobby becomes a way of meditating, focusing and concentrating happen naturally, because it's not a job, nor a duty, you really want to do what you're doing!

THE SOUL IN WOODWORKING, PHOTOGRAPHY, SILVERSMITHING, AND BUILDING CHOPPERS

When you're working on a hobby, meditation can last for hours. Or it may peak in a sudden flash of insight—when you're doing what

3.8 HOBBIES & CRAFTS

you love, a warm feeling comes over you, you get a sense of total peace, and for a moment you know deep down how lucky you are, thankful for the opportunity to be doing what you love doing—and in those beautiful moments your craft is transformed into the perfect meditation. We've all experienced it. Here are several people telling us in their own words about this magical way of meditating:

George Nakashima in *The Soul of a Tree, a Woodworker's Reflections:* "A tree provides perhaps our most intimate contact with nature. A tree sits like an avatar, and embodiment of the immutable, far beyond the pains of man ... We woodworkers have the audacity to shape timber from these noble trees. In a sense, it is our Karma Yoga, the path of action we must take to our union with the Divine."

Bernard Bernstein in *Silver-Smithing* by Finegold & Seitz: "Silversmithing is a craft with a rich and ancient tradition and, in this technologically overprivileged society, it is a kind of economic anachronism. However, it provides its practitioners with immense personal rewards, not the least of which are the mesmerizing, possibly meditative pleasures of hammering out form for hours at a time."

Linda Kohanov: *"The Tao of Equus* essentially translates as 'the way of the horse,' while emphasizing the healing and transformational qualities of this path. Interacting with these animals can be immensely therapeutic physically, mentally, and spiritually, helping people reawaken long-forgotten abilities that are capable of healing the imbalances of modern life."

Tom Ang in *The Tao of Photography:* "You can learn to 'see' a picture before you take it; and when you acquire this ability, you will spend less time looking for photographs. They'll discover themselves for you. You will then not need to seek; you will find." And most other photographers agree. For example, Joy Ribisi says: "Photography is meditation. I am able to leave the shell of my body and express my thoughts, my sights, my emotions."

Jesse James, the world's leading builder of "choppers," customized *Easy Rider* motorcycles, first as a hobby. When the brash tattooed James talks about his sculptural beauties, you sense he's working in a meditative state that the Zen masters would envy: "Success for me is to be able to come here to West Coast Choppers and to work hard, in peace and make beautiful stuff."

NFL DEFENSIVE GIANT LOVES NEEDLEPOINT

By now you know the range of hobbies as a way of meditation is without limit—it's whatever *suits your personality.* Jesse James the chopper guy is a bad-ass, my-way-or-the-highway kind of personality: "You know those needlepoint wall hangings that say 'Home Sweet Home'? I just had my friend's mom, who is really good at those, make one for my house. It says, 'Go F--- Yourself,' but it looks exactly like a nice needlepoint."

Rosey Grier is also a mean, in-your-face guy. Back in the sixties Rosey was a star Los Angeles Rams lineman, anchoring the Fearsome Foursome Rams defensive line. After he retired from making life miserable for opposing quarterbacks, he became a movie actor, then a minister, and later wrote *Rosey Grier's Needle Point for Men.* You hear right—needlepoint! In his book Rosey tells of an insurance executive, a real estate broker, an international banker and a stock broker member of the NYSE, all active needlepointers.

HOBBIES HELP YOU "ZONE-OUT" OPENING YOUR MIND TO THE INNER CREATOR

In Dr. Herbert Benson's most recent book, *The Breakout Principle,* he tells us that Oscar-winning Russell Crowe, fashion designer Bob Mackie and television network executive Stu Bloomberg are also members of this elite "male knitting underground" because it's great stress relief.

One leading management consultant tells how he uses knitting to come up with solutions to sticky business problems: "The insight has to come from the outside. It's absolutely essential for me to get away from my job and coworkers. Put myself in a completely different space. The best way for me to shift gears is needlepoint."

How does it work? Dr. Benson says this businessman "found that when he was working on a background canvas, with only one color

3.8 HOBBIES & CRAFTS

and one type of stitch, the work was highly repetitive. Row after row, he executed exactly the same finger movements. As a result, he could 'zone out.' Most important of all, he could break all previous trains of thought—and let his mind wander and hover freely, over this and that."

And then, as he let go and moved away from everything into another mental space, he created a mental vacuum—that's when he was open and new insights could come in, after surrendering to another reality.

MYSTERIOUS LINKS BETWEEN HOBBIES'N'CRAFTS, CREATIVITY, MEDITATION AND SPIRITUALITY

Real men do yoga and needlepoint, flower arranging and other outside-the-box hobbies. Why? Because "most anything can be meditative" says Peg Baim, a colleague of Dr. Benson, founder of the Harvard Mind/Body Institute. Baim was quoted in Bernadette Murphy's *Zen & the Art of Knitting: Exploring the Links Between Knitting, Spirituality & Creativity:* "When people meditate or participate in a meditative activity like knitting ... they increase their creativity, shut off their spatial awareness and time orientation, and they may experience oneness, unity, expansion, feelings of hope, and awe."

Don't get us wrong, we're not suggesting you take up needlepoint, any more than silver-smithing, woodworking, horseback riding, or build choppers. The point is, you begin with what turns you on, something that makes you want to "work hard, in peace and make beautiful stuff." You already know what that is in your heart, and you're already doing it. Here's a little checklist of other possibilities of hobbies that can become meditations:

Crafting hard materials: Manual labor is now missing from so much of what us workers do in today's high-tech society, which is why so many people crave hobbies that demand hands-on physical work: auto and boat restoration and racing, home renovations and cabinetry, pottery making and ceramics, glassblowing and leather working, model making for airplanes and trains.

Collectibles: Stamps and coins, as a kid I fell in love with the sheer beauty of these miniature artworks, vicariously traveling the world and learning history. My son had a huge comic book collection, later became a graphics illustrator. An actor friend traveled the country collecting 19th century glass. Another collects guitars. We all know enthusiasts avid about collecting baseball cards, records, clocks, salt shakers and autographs. Others collect and restore antiques and art of all kinds. I recall reading about how a charming little librarian and her husband amassed America's premiere collection of minimalist art on a minimal budget. All are doing what they love.

Artistic crafts: Painting, drawing and sketching may expand into a line of handmade cards or some specialty in the printing arts such as book binding, calligraphy, origami, collages, montages. Another alternative is toy-making, puppets, dolls, teddy bears. Floral arranging. Making confectioneries, candles, or soap. Other possibilities: Weaving, fabric making and fashion design. Jewelry and gem designing, bead stringing. Shortly before I started at Morgan Stanley a male professional left to create a line of sculptural silver belt buckles that were being sold in upscale Madison Avenue shops.

THE ULTIMATE MEDITATION
SHARING A CHILD'S FAVORITE HOBBY

And forget about all the gender stuff: Rams lineman Rosey Grier (needlepoint) and Cy Young Award Winning pitcher Barry Zito (yoga) have blown apart male-female stereotypes. Gender considerations shouldn't influence your choice of hobbies. It's far more important that you simple tap into the creative child within you—and what better way than to help a child with *their* favorite hobby.

If you've ever shared a creative hobby with your kids you know exactly what I mean. For a little kid, creativity, crafts and hobbies are natural ways to meditate—*except they don't put those kind of fancy mental labels on what they're doing, they just do them and have fun.*

3.8 HOBBIES & CRAFTS

For example, go pick up a simple book like the Better Homes & Gardens, *501 Fun-to-Make Family Crafts.* The book is loaded with creative, fun stuff to do with kids for seasonal events, holidays, birthdays, parties. And each time you're cutting out a snowflake or heart, pasting up a paper turkey, or coloring Easter eggs, meditate for a moment on what it all means to you and to that wonderful little child.

Discover what it's like to create like a little kid. Then come back and live with that same feeling in your own hobbies—because that spirit is what every meditation is about.

THE CREATIVITY ZONE

AN "ARTIST DATE"
AS MEDITATION

*The capacity for silence—a deep, creative awareness
of one's inner truth—is what distinguishes us as human.
All of us, however ordinary or flawed, have at heart
a seemingly bound-less longing for fulfillment ...
Silence is a paradox, intensely there
and with equal intensity, not there ...
There is nothing to say, nothing even to experience
in any words that sound impressive,
yet the looking never wearies.*
Sister Wendy's
Book of Meditations

HAD ENOUGH? STRESSED to the max? Office driving you nuts. Some business problem you're working on has you totally frustrated. You can't seem to get an important project off the ground. Your brain's locked up. Nothing's working. You need solutions now, a new idea, a brainstorm—but drawing blanks? Running up cul du sacs, into dead-ends! You're exhausted, can't think straight!!

Sound familiar? It happens to everyone in business at some point. You're trying hard—*probably too hard for too long*—and it's not working. Happened to me so many times in New York City and Los Angeles, with Corporate America blue chips, in the investment banking business of Wall Street. You're running on empty ... your brain freezes ... locks up ... grinds to a halt!

3.9 AN "ARTIST DATE"

WHEN YOU CAN'T FIND THE SOLUTION
PLAY HIDE'N'SEEK—LET IT FIND YOU!

This simple meditation technique works like a charm. And it's one of the best for anyone in the workaday world. Think of it as an adult version of hide'n'seek. You've probably already tried it without thinking of it as meditation. It's worked for me many times, and I'll bet for millions of others on Wall Street and throughout Corporate America. It happens so naturally, you just flow with it.

Here's the simple three-step meditation process in a nutshell, with a little explanation to help you understand why this kind of meditation is so effective and powerful in solving business problems and reducing stress. Follow these three simple steps and you'll get the most out of it, and I'll bet you start doing it on a regular basis when your brain locks and you're stressed out:

STEP ONE
STOP WHATEVER YOU'RE DOING! NOW!

Stop right now! Stop everything, turn the computer off—get out of the office! Right in the middle of the day? Yes! You must interrupt the obsessive ruminating that dug your brain into a deep rut. And yes, you will probably feel guilty, like you're escaping from reality, or wasting company time, just procrastinating, indecisive, or a loser because you can't do the job in front of you. Self-criticism goes with the territory, it's natural and expected. Stop anyway. Get out of the office, leave, go, right now!

STEP TWO
DON'T THINK! DO SOMETHING SPONTANEOUS!

Do something impulsive, unpredictable, unplanned, unusual, weird, odd, inspiring, nutty, artistic and creative! Anything other than what you're doing! Something that sounds like it's coming from deep within you—a voice, muse, spirit, artist, child, whatever, even if you're not really sure what, listen to it. And when you do it, shift gears—you should get totally and absolutely and completely into whatever you're going to do, and exit the scene of the problem.

STEP THREE
GET OUT OF THE OFFICE! YES, ESCAPE! GO!

It could be as simple as a slow walk through a new exhibit at the museum. An opening at an offbeat art gallery. Just sit and contemplate one work of art. Or go sit by a waterfall in a favorite vest pocket park and read a novel. Or work your way through the great masterpieces in *Sister Wendy's Book of Meditations,* stopping occasionally to explore what art means in your life.

Your meditation could also be a short trip to the local library, or your familiar book store—grab a few magazines that you've *never* opened before. *Yes, never!* Read them over a latte in their coffeeshop. Buy one. Maybe take in a movie, or just watch some animals in the zoo, street musicians, birds on a park pond. You might go shopping, buy a surprise gift for someone you've never given a gift. Do something unusual, pleasurable, and spontaneously.

PROVE THAT YOU REALLY CAN
MAKE ANYTHING INTO A MEDITATION

Isn't that what meditation is all about? Remember, anything can be a meditation—you simply focus on one thing and one thing only, and cut out all the distractions, like the problem you can't solve because your brain locked up.

Except here you're reversing the steps: First, you stop and get away from all the distractions of your office, all the stuff that has your brain locked up. Then, you focus on something else—*anything*—something different from what you've been focusing on, something creative. That's your meditation: Focusing on the new thing while putting time and distance between the frustration and the next creation.

HERE'S WHY AN "ARTIST DATE" WORKS

Why does this work to reduce stress and help you find creative solutions? That's very simple, and once you understand why this works you'll be able to do it more consciously and more frequently in the future. And as paradoxical as it sounds, you'll want to program

3.9 AN "ARTIST DATE"

these unexpected creative journeys into your workday knowing they will increase your productivity in the long run.

When Julia Cameron's book *The Artist's Way* hit the stores in the early nineties, she gave millions of stressed-out people permission to escape the pressures, stop in the middle of a busy workday, and take a long break. Cameron's the genius who identified the "artist date."

This is probably not new to you. It's certainly not rocket science. And you don't need a mega-ton MRI to test the idea. If you've ever made up some excuse and snuck out of the office in the middle of a stressful day after your brain locked up, as I often did, you know exactly what I'm talking about.

YOU'RE STUCK IN THE "WRONG BRAIN!"

Cameron put on paper what we've been doing all along. This is how the brain works psychologically, and naturally—your brain has two hemispheres that operate like networked computers, with each handling different tasks.

The Logic Brain: The left-brain is the rational brain, the worker-bee. Cameron calls it the "logic brain." This half of your brain is happiest and most efficient when working like an unemotional computer, thinking objectively and logically. It loves analyzing, counting, planning things step-by-step, verbalizing procedures.

However, if family problems are affecting you emotionally, or you're tired, overloaded and behind schedule, for example, stress builds, frustration takes over and this amazing left-brain computer will lock up. You can't think straight—*so you have to reboot your "computer!"*

The Artist Brain: The other hemisphere of the brain is the creator, the inventor, the innovator—it thinks out-of-sequence, in images, ideas, dreams, metaphors and concepts, always synthesizing, searching for patterns, making connections, linking the pieces.

This Inner Artist naturally functions outside the everyday "real" world of business facts, scientific data and concrete evidence, envisioning and creating new realities. Unfortunately, over-loading the logical left-brain "Thinker" will also shut down the right-brain creative hemisphere.

SCHEDULING REGULAR ARTIST DATES

When your brain locks up, you can pry open the lock by taking your inner creative source on an "artist date!" Yes, I know this sounds bizarre, weird, even childish—especially for some hot-shot executive, banker or attorney in a three-piece suit and a corner office on the 43rd floor of a skyscraper … but trust me, it works, it's fun, it's productive! And it's a very simple:

So you're blocked: Time to take your Inner Artist on a date. "But what exactly is an artist date?" asks Cameron. Well, here's her structured version: "An artist date is a block of time, perhaps two hours weekly, especially set aside and committed to nurturing your creative consciousness, your inner artist. In its most primary form, the artist date is an excursion, a play date that you preplan and defend against all interlopers. You cannot take anyone on this artist date but you and your inner artist, a.k.a. your creative child. That means no lovers, friends, spouses, children—no taggers-on—of any stripe."

That's the structured version. A great way to chill out, get back in touch with your Inner Creator, and restart the creative juices on a regular basis.

OLD MOVIES, BOWLING, ANTIQUE SHOPPING, ETHNIC FOOD, GOSPEL SINGING & MUSEUMS

Here's another approach: You can use this same basic meditation anytime, impulsively—when you're working in the middle of the day and your brain freezes. When you know you can't solve an important problem and you're certain you're wasting your time.

Just say to your Inner Artist: "Hey, let's get out of here. Let's go on a date, right now, this very minute, stop what we're doing because not much is happening anyway, quietly sneak out of the office and go on a date." *Then head for the nearest exit, fast!* And don't think about it for long because your logical brain is certain to try talking you out of it!

3.9 AN "ARTIST DATE"

Cameron's description gets to the core of the psychology here: "Your artist is a child. Time with a parent matters more than the money spent. A visit to a great junk store, a solo trip to the beach, an old movie seen alone together, a visit to an aquarium or an art gallery ... a sortie out to a strange church to hear gospel music, to an ethnic neighborhood to taste foreign sights and sounds—your artist might enjoy any of these. Or your artist might enjoy bowling."

IT'S NOT WHAT YOU DO JUŞT THAT YOU ARE DOING IT

But remember, what you do on your artist date is not as important as doing it. Get away from the frustrations and distraction, let go and relax, then focus on some little adventure with your inner creative artist. It'll work anytime, and you'll quickly discover that these times of "doing nothing" will increase your productivity as well as your peace of mind in the long-run—and that, my friends, is what this unique meditation is all about.

THE CREATIVITY ZONE

THE ART of "DOING NOTHING"
AS MEDITATION

> *Anytime you either slow down, resist a task, or invent some*
> *inane reason for getting behind schedule, pay special attention.*
> *Take these organizational lapses as an indication that*
> *you are on the verge of some major breakthrough.*
> *You are probably entering a zone of creativity.*
> *Don't intervene with the process at hand.*
> Veronique Vienne
> *The Art of Imperfection*

EVERYONE LOVES THIS way of meditating. Start by asking yourself: Where do our creative ideas come from? Are you the creator, the source, the master of your own fate? Or do creative ideas come to us from somewhere else while we are "sitting quietly, doing nothing," as Eastern mystics suggest?

Are some mortals—Michelangelo, Thomas Edison, James Michener, Picasso and Alfred Hitchcock—born idea generators? How much depends on what we do with our creative talents, designing buildings and inventions, writing historical novels, creating works of art and film? Are we the creators or just vehicles for some universal Creator, the Mastermind as Napoleon Hill calls it, a power that works through us in mysterious ways?

In *Success Through a Positive Mental Attitude* Napoleon Hill relates a wonderful little story about an interview he had with Dr. Elmer Gates, a scientist who owns a couple hundred patents on his inventions.

4.0 THE ART OF "DOING NOTHING"

"SEEING" NEW IDEAS—SITTING IN THE DARK

When Hill arrived, Gates' secretary apologized and said he'd have to wait, perhaps a few hours—her boss was "sitting for ideas." So Hill sat patiently and waited. When Gates finally emerged from his sound-proof meditation chamber, as we'd call it today, Gates "explained that when he was unable to obtain an answer to a problem, he went into the room, sat down, turned off the lights, and engaged in deep concentration. He applied the success principle of controlled attention, asking his subconscious mind to give him an answer."

Hill wrote that in the fifties, before the meditation practices of Zen Buddhism became popular in America. So while his *Positive Mental Attitude* language reflects the thinking of the Western business world, there is, nevertheless, a strange similarity between Gates' scientific approach and the meditation practices of Eastern mystics expressed in the 13th century Zen poem: "Sitting quietly, doing nothing, spring comes and the grass grows."

A KICK IN THE PANTS, A WHACK ON THE HEAD AND YOU'RE THINKING OUTSIDE-THE-BOX!

"There's no right way to be creative," says Roger von Oech in *A Kick in the Seat of the Pants*, "each creative thinker has his own style." He should know, von Oech is president of Creative Think, a leading consultant to Corporate America. But in spite of our differences, we can improve our odds of generating better creative solutions.

How? By using the kind of tools he discusses in *Kick* and his other classic, *A Whack on the Side of the Head: How You Can Be More Creative*. As von Oech puts it, when it comes to creativity, we're our own biggest enemy: "When there is a need to 'think something different,' our own attitudes can get in the way. I call these attitudes *mental locks.*" Solution? If you can't forget about them, whack yourself on the side of the head and "dislodge the presuppositions that hold the locks in place."

In today's high-tech world, ideas create wealth and power. Look at who's on top of the Forbes 400 and the Fortune 500. Thinking "different" is also the key to individual wealth building says Thomas Stanley in *The Millionaire Mind:* "What do most millionaires tell me they learned?" he asks rhetorically. "They learned to: Think differently from the crowd." As a result, his entire book was "designed around a central theme: It pays to be different."

IN TODAY'S MEGA-PRESSURE 24/7 WORLD STOP TRYING—SIT QUIETLY—DO NOTHING

Every creative thinker in the business world has their own style, whether you're an entrepreneur on Main Street, working inside Corporate America, or a dealmaker on Wall Street. Some of us are born innovators, and yet all of us can sharpen our creative edge. Persistence helps: It did for Thomas Edison when he was inventing the light bulb. Others get it in a sudden inspirational flash. Still others, like Gates, came up with creative solutions while "sitting quietly, doing nothing," meditating in his dark, quiet sanctuary.

And yet, while there may be no one right way to think creatively in today's super-rational, high pressure, competitive business world, creativity often comes only when we stop trying so hard ... even stop trying altogether ... take a break and go to a movie ... walk around the block ... play Ping-Pong ... go exercise at the gym ... or think outside-the-box in bizarre, whimsical ways ... be a child, play games with make-believe friends.

"For a child, doing nothing doesn't mean being inactive, it means doing something that doesn't have a name," says Veronique Vienne in *The Art of Doing Nothing.* "You can recapture that moment of utter serenity simply by refusing to put a label on everything you do. Practice doing 'nothing' ... by uncluttering your mind."

LESS IS MORE

Meditation is becoming increasingly popular because today's business world is so out of balance. We have forgotten that, as with music, the quality of the creation is often measured by the silences between the notes.

Elmer Gates understood the need to balance active thinking with periods of "doing nothing," he was like a Tibetan monk. Today's business arena is so overwhelmed by a relentless rapid-fire barrage of loud notes that we have to go out of our way if we hope to program

4.0 THE ART OF "DOING NOTHING"

more silence in between the notes—that is, more time for the creative child within us to "do nothing," as only a child can.

TRUST THE SIGNALS
YOU WILL KNOW WHEN TO "DO NOTHING"

And you will know instinctively when it's time to do nothing: "Anytime you either slow down, resist a task, or invent some inane reason for getting behind schedule, pay special attention," says Vienne Veronique in *The Art of Imperfection.* Trust yourself:

"Take these organizational lapses as an indication that you are on the verge of some major breakthrough. You are probably entering a zone of creativity. Don't intervene with the process at hand ... Be just as patient with yourself ... Heedless bustling is evidence that you are on a holding pattern, waiting for the next available landing strip in your brain. ... According to productivity experts, taking frequent breaks yield higher profits."

Listen closely and trust your creative insights. "You are at the center of a formidable information network," says Vienne in The *Art of the Moment:* "Moment by moment a sixth sense keeps you updated on your inner state, your thoughts, your feelings. You instantly know everything there is to know about yourself." Trust the signals, you will know when to bull ahead—and when it's time to "sit quietly and do nothing."

AN ACCIDENTAL TRIP INTO ENLIGHTENMENT
WHERE FIFTY BUCKS IS BETTER THAN A MILLION

Creative insights, brainstorms, an epiphany, aha moments, enlightenment, call it whatever you want, many of us are searching for this elusive, intangible something. And whatever it is, we want more of it! Vienne described this amazing search in rather simple language:

"What is enlightenment? ... Hundreds of Zen stories tell of how monks failed to attain satori after decades of practice, only to stumble on it by accident. The anecdotes are interpreted as evidence that you can only prepare for spiritual change, you cannot control it.

"Reaching enlightenment is a bit like winning the lottery—not a million-dollar bonanza, mind you, just fifty bucks. The odds are in your favor. Years later, you'll laugh remembering how sudden yet how anti-climatic the event really was. You'll wonder why it wasn't more emotional or dramatic.

"You probably weren't meditating. Chances are you were waiting for the light to change at an intersection, or looking out the window while talking on the phone, or washing dishes after a party. You were not prepared for it. No one can expect the unexpected—no one is every ready to be enlightened.

"Your moment of enlightenment came packaged as a thought bubble. On a scale of one to ten, it was probably a number four insight ….

"Enlightenment is just another word for feeling comfortable with being a completely ordinary person. At long last, the unexceptional seems extraordinary enough: a puddle of water, a child running after a bird, the peaceful hum of your computer—and you, in the midst of it all, with your unvarnished self-image. The charade is over and a painful existential headache is gone. You are not a perfect human being—far from it—but your mind is clear. For the first time, you feel unflustered, alert, and ready to go."

WHEN DOING NOTHING—JUST DO NOTHING! LET "NOTHING" DO "SOMETHING" FOR YOU

When you get this, when you truly understand that doing nothing is the natural way to enlightenment in an everyday world loaded with problems, then it should be very easy for you to understand that doing *anything* can be a meditation! When it happens for you, just remember, there are few if any enlightened beings in the world, only enlightened moments. So enjoy doing nothing, and stay open, so that "nothing" can do something for you.

THE RELATIONSHIP ZONE
10 ways to meditate—sharing your values

4.1—**MASTERMIND RELATIONSHIPS**

4.2—**LEADERSHIP**

4.3—**PUBLIC SERVICE**

4.4—**TEACHING, COACHING, MENTORING**

4.5—**SELF-HELP PROGRAMS**

4.6—**COUNSELING SESSIONS**

4.7—**RELIGIOUS CELEBRATIONS**

4.8—**PILGRIMAGES & JOURNEYS**

4.9—**INTIMATE RELATIONSHIPS**

5.0—**PARENTING & THE FAMILY**

THE RELATIONSHIP ZONE
OF MEDITATION

*Only when I left the monastery and returned to
the life of a wage-earner did it occur to me that
for years my meditation practice had been exactly like
one of those little bonsai trees, an exotic specimen,
raised under carefully controlled conditions,
and pruned in accordance with the aesthetic
of an exacting discipline, but essentially an indoor miniature
that would not survive in the open as an ordinary tree.*
Clark Strand,
The Wooden Bowl;
A Simple Meditation for Everyday Life

*You're at work and there's so much going on
around you and you have such an opportunity to
be distracted or lash out—that, to me, is where
my practice of meditation has really blossomed.*
Elizabeth Lesser
The New American Spirituality

IN EACH OF the prior three zones—mental, sports and creativity—meditation is primarily an individual activity focused on your personal needs. In this fourth zone you'll find ways to meditate in everyday situations, with people at work, socially, and with your family—it could be a business lunch, mentoring a young executive, chairing a civic activity, coaching your son's soccer team, sharing an intimate moment with your spouse. Remember, you can turn any experience into a meditation, anything. It's up to you.

Meditating in the Relationship Zone means putting the golden rule into action, making it part of your daily life, where deeply-held personal values inspire you to help other people, satisfy their needs, accomplish their goals.

Being of service to others is perhaps the one single message common to the teachings of all great spiritual traditions throughout history and across all cultures—it is also the one experience that gives each of us opportunities to transform our everyday lives into meditation.

THE OPPORTUNITIES ARE EVERYWHERE EVERY DAY ... ALL DAY ... WITH EVERYONE

Take a moment, look around, your world is filled with many big and small ways to meditate throughout the day—in your relationships with loved ones and friends, in your business and social network, in public affairs, in your contacts with strangers on the street, in stores, the elevator, on the phone, online. Everyday we have an endless flow of opportunities to meditate with other people, as we work and play and socialize.

The key: Simply shift your focus. In a brief moment you can transform any relationship into a meditative experience. *Remember the basic rules and focus on other people, ask yourself how you can be of service to them!* That's what's so great about this simple approach to meditating—you call the shots, you're the boss. You're in charge of making whatever you're doing a meditation, while reducing stress and increasing your energy—it's an easy decision!

Start by looking around today. Keep it simple. The opportunities are everywhere. Here are ten ways of meditating in this Relationship Zone, suggestions about how you can blend your world of individual meditating with your relationships in business, family and socially. Remember, this is highly personal area. In the final analysis, *your task is to find ways that work for you.*

ONE
BUSINESS MASTERMINDS AS MEDITATION

Here's one my wife and I have been practicing every week for many years. I first read about the "Mastermind" in one of the first motivational books I ever read, the early classics of Napoleon Hill, *Think & Grow Rich,* and *Success Through a Positive Mental Attitude.* Both were inspired by Hill's mentor, billionaire Andrew Carnegie.

Hill's Mastermind concept is the single most powerful of his "Secrets of Success" principles. In today's business world you might call it networking, building relationships. But it is far more, far deeper. Hill describes a Mastermind as "an alliance of two or more minds blended in a spirit of perfect harmony and co-operating for the attainment of a single purpose."

An alliance, harmony, focus, purpose: That sure sounds like an ideal and effective relationship. That's also what every meditation is about. In other words, focusing on a single purpose makes a Mastermind group a natural opportunity for meditation.

For example, Andrew Carnegie said his Mastermind was his fifty-man staff. Carnegie even "attributed his entire fortune to the power he accumulated through his Mastermind." Today we can see Mastermind groups operating in our lives in so many ways, evolving naturally. Although typically known by other names, the idea is what's important, people in action, working together, in harmony, focused on a common goal. Remember, meditation is that simple.

IN GLOBAL FORUMS AND QUIET LUNCHES

Mastermind groups take many forms. Friendships like the one between Warren Buffett and Bill Gates. A retreat for your company's top executives. Or the annual World Economic Forum in Davos, Switzerland attended by leaders from government, business, academia, religion, the media and others from more than a hundred countries to support the goals of an organization "committed to the improvement of the state of the world."

It may be as simple as a next lunch date with a close friend and confident. A meeting with a mentor is also an obvious Mastermind—

an opportunity to share values, challenge and debate, plan and support—with someone you trust.

Can a Mastermind group operate solely on a commercial level? Perhaps, but Hill says all the Mastermind groups he researched drew their energy and strength from a source beyond the commercial arena, and even beyond the individual people in the group: "No two minds ever come together without, thereby, creating a third, invisible, intangible force which may be likened to a third mind."

THE POWER OF A MASTERMIND NETWORK

Moreover, as Hill got to know each of the hundreds of successful men who helped him develop his Science of Success principles, he "discovered that *each of them* had received guidance from unknown sources." Every one of them admitted that a higher power was guiding them personally in their business ventures, even though they may have been unable to identify the source of the power.

We saw an example of this guidance in action in *The Relaxation Response*. Benson identifies Sir John Marks Templeton, the founder of Templeton Funds, as one of his mentors and supporters. Templeton ran his financial empire and his life as a Mastermind group, there was no separation between the secular and spiritual, the financial and metaphysical.

Templeton opened every business meeting with a prayer: "If you begin with prayer, you will think more clearly and make fewer mistakes." In fact, "whatever you do in life—whether you get married, bring a case to a law court, operate on a child, or buy a stock—you should open with prayer."

THINKING OUTSIDE THE MEDITATION BOX

Once you begin thinking outside the box about what can or can't be a "meditation," you come to realize that in fact anything really can become a meditation, *anything* you're doing during the business day—whether leading, supporting your colleagues, or working in a team. You soon understand that a Mastermind group is a perfect way for hard-nosed executives to meditate with others in today's stressful business world, without making a big deal of it.

THE RELATIONSHIP ZONE

Napoleon Hill discovered that whenever two or more executives joined forces in a common purpose, they were guided by powerful, yet unseen forces that make them far more powerful than each working separately. Together they can go beyond what we know as synergism in the business world, to become a team led by a third mind—the Mastermind—and from this experience you can create a powerful meditation, and grow rich in spirit and in fact. It works.

TWO
LEADERSHIP AS MEDITATION

We can easily accept that the Dalai Lama is a leader, even when he's sitting in silent meditation. But what about business and financial leaders? We see them as action-oriented, focused on money, obsessed about the bottom line. Somehow the Zen principle that by "sitting quietly, doing nothing, spring will come, and earnings will grow" doesn't quite fit the image of a leader on Wall Street or in Corporate America.

On the other hand, we know that many business and financial executives do meditate while, for example, jogging or surfing, practicing Aikido, or playing a musical instrument. And many like Carnegie and Templeton try to live with this mindset every day and everywhere, in the boardroom, customers' offices, clients, suppliers and employees, and in meetings with investors—they know that somehow they're guided by unknown and mysterious sources.

Aaron Feuerstein is example of this type of leadership character, a man whose actions speak louder rather than some fancy corporate mission statement. Feuerstein is the owner and CEO of New England's largest textile mill, the manufacturer of Polartec. Feuerstein is a gentle man in his seventies who loved working. When the day was over, he preferred a quiet evening at home reading poetry and sharing inspirational literature with his wife.

Feuerstein became a national hero. The "Mensch of Malden Mills," as he was known, was thrust in the national spotlight when fires destroyed his textile factories in the late nineties. Instead of taking the insurance money and retiring, he not only rebuilt, he continued paying all 3,000 employees for the three months it took to get back into operation, because it was "the right thing to do." Feuerstein would probably not describe his way of life as a meditation any more than he wanted to be called a hero.

And yet, in the larger context—*where anything can be a meditation ... where results count more than rituals ... where you can even be meditating without knowing it ... where the trick is focusing on whatever you're doing at the moment*—the selfless actions of Feuerstein are a far more powerful meditation than any monk passively sitting in meditation for decades.

THREE
PUBLIC SERVICE AS MEDITATION

Successful business leaders are often known for their tough exteriors. Meditation and spirituality aren't highlighted in their job description. Yes, it is okay to attend Sunday church services, even serve meals in a skid row soup kitchen on Thanksgiving. But when you're negotiating a merger, closing a big sale, appeasing disgruntled investors or disciplining a key employee, you better be focused, disciplined and tough. Let your guard down and the sharks will eat you alive.

Executives often show their softer side in other ways, such as public service, through volunteer work in charities and civic organizations. They balance toughness, compassion and service for the greater good, and often find that it's good for business too.

One example was reported *Fortune* magazine, in an article about Hank Paulson, CEO of Goldman Sachs, a $45 billion Wall Street investment banking powerhouse with 20,000 employees worldwide. Having worked for his arch-rival, Morgan Stanley, I was especially intrigued by Paulson's ability to balance business and public service.

Paulson is not only a tough executive—"carved features without a hint of softness ... a really, really ruthless competitor"—he has "another equally intense existence, as a lover of wildlife and protector of the environment." He also serves as co-chair of the $3.3 billion Nature Conservancy, the world's largest nonprofit environmental organization.

As a young man Paulson wanted to become a forest ranger. Today he's living that dream. His travels take him and his supporters in the Conservancy to Indonesia's rain forests, China's mountain reserves, the coral reefs of Palau in the Western Pacific, and other endangered areas of Asia.

Paulson says: "It isn't like I'm trying to do good, this is really fun for me." And yet the guy *is* doing a lot of good, driven by a deep conviction that saving the environment is a "race against time, the ultimate global issue." Meditation? Yes, a life filled with such intense focus and passion at work and in public service is a perfect meditation.

MAKING A DIFFERENCE IN THE WORLD

Tex Gunning, president of Unilever Bestfoods Asia is another example. Gunning is an economist by training according to an article in *What is Enlightenment?* magazine. Early in his career he became a "restructuring" expert—a corporate hatchet man. But in midlife, he decided he no longer wanted to "keep sacking and keep restructuring and keep cutting costs."

Gunning had an epiphany: "I didn't want to live a life creating an illusion of meaningfulness while deep in my heart I knew that every five seconds there is a child dying." He decided he would "make a difference in the lives of unbelievably poor children in Asia. Their suffering is just unimaginable. I said to myself, I have no choice." Unilever backed him and since then he's started profitable food businesses in fifteen countries. This is meditation in action, different and perhaps more effective than retreating into a monastery.

FOUR
MENTORING & COACHING AS MEDITATION

Many executives serve as mentors for the next generation of leaders. For some it may be as simple as coaching your son's Little League team, perhaps scoutmaster of a local troop, or a big brother, a role model for a disadvantaged kid, helping him build confidence and find direction in his life.

THE RELATIONSHIP ZONE

Not all executives will be in the league of powerplayers as Goldman Sachs' Paulson. But that didn't stop Morgan Stanley vice president Claudine McIntee. Here's her story from *The Corporate Athlete:*

McIntee says "I live in a suburb outside of New York City, and every morning when I travel in, I pray. It gets me focused and centered for the day. Every Wednesday, I also read to a fourth-grade student from an inner city school for an hour and a half, trying to be a role-model for her … It is really very rewarding, because when I am crazy or I get worked up over something at work, I walk to see this kid and talk to her … there were people in my life who have given to me. I feel a sense of responsibility to give back to others."

Mentoring, coaching and teaching are a big part of being an effective leader, and a measure of a person's true character. In these kinds of relationships you're bringing the best out of a person so they can become more effective, productive, and better equipped to make independent decisions and take on the world themselves.

In every one of these situations your role as a mentor, coach and teacher is a perfect opportunity to get out of yourself and meditate along with the other person—by focusing solely on helping them. And the great thing about this way of meditating is that you don't have to tell them you're meditating at all, or even label what you're doing "meditation," to anyone. You just do it.

FIVE
SELF-HELP PROGRAMS AS MEDITATION

Meditation is one of the key operating principles of the Twelve-Step self-help programs. For example, their 11th Step reads: "Sought through prayer and meditation to improve our conscious contact with God as we understood Him, praying only for knowledge of His will for us and the power to carry it out."

These self-help programs play a huge role in the lives of many people. Various estimates suggest that between one third and one half of all Americans are either directly or indirectly affected by the disease of chemical depencency, affecting all demographic, ethnic and economic groups equally.

So it should come as no surprise to find out that many corporate executives, Wall Street dealmakers, and successful professionals are already members of these Twelve-Step groups, protected by their commitment to anonymity. And as part of their recovery program I know many of these men and women not only meditate regularly, it is a big part of their lives.

Moreover, they often meditate collectively. Earlier, as a crisis consultant, I worked with hundreds of recovering individuals who went through The Betty Ford Center. These included executives, professionals, doctors, athletes, entertainers, celebrities and several members of royalty. I could see how they meditated during group sessions, by focusing on a particular topic, or saying prayers together.

SIX
COUNSELING & THERAPY AS MEDITATION

We already know that seventy to ninety percent of all doctors' visits are stress-related. A third have high blood pressure. We also know that more than half of all Americans see counselors and go into therapy sometime during the course of their lives, to handle stresses of all kinds—the loss of a loved one, health problems, bankruptcies, job losses, addictions and much more. There is a special bond during these sessions, we are meditating together.

Earlier, for fourteen years before I started working as a professional career and crisis consultant, I was on the other side of the couch struggling through a long "dark night of the soul." I needed help and got it from all kinds of therapists, counselors, psychologists and psychiatrists. And on occasion I also got advice from unconventional sources: astrologers, psychics, Tarot card readers, numerologists, palmists, hypnotists, New Age gurus, healers, I Ching masters and for a few years I worked with a neo-Reichian Sikh.

During this long dark night I became increasingly aware that whatever meditation was, it was happening right there during each one of these sessions. Today I know there is actually nothing unusual about seeing the therapeutic relationship as a meditation: As I learned much later, the goal of Buddhist insight meditation, Vipassana, is identical to Western psychotherapy, both seeking greater awareness, higher consciousness and enlightenment.

SEVEN
RELIGIOUS CELEBRATIONS AS MEDITATION

Religious celebrations, rituals and services are probably the world's most natural opportunity for group meditation. The architecture, the ritual, the pageantry, scriptural readings, music, singing—whether it's the Pope saying Mass on New Year's Eve, or a Mass in the tiny crypt below St. Francis' Basilica in Assisi, a Greek wedding or evangelist meeting, a Bar Mitzvah or gospel choir. Every one is a natural meditation. Religious celebrations are a time to come together, to pray, to rejoice, to cry, to meditate, to celebrate life.

Like so many going through a dark night of the soul, I went on a search through many spiritual traditions—Quaker meetings, Science of Mind lectures, Navaho sweat lodges, Yoga practice, Sufi dancing, est Forums, za-zen meditation, and many other ways to celebrate the spirit in each of us. So different, and yet so much alike.

Near the end of my first Quaker meeting I actually did see "tongues of fire" coming from the tops of the heads of the congregation. Only later did I learn that this was a core belief of the Quakers, and yet at the time it seemed so natural and so real, no different than being in a sweat lodge or yoga class.

From my early days as an Irish Catholic altar boy, to serving Mass for Marine chaplains in Korean huts, to all these celebrations in so many cultures and spiritual traditions around the world I came to understand that every religious celebration is a meditation.

EIGHT
PILGRIMAGES & JOURNEYS AS MEDITATION

Ancient and modern masters often remind us that life is a journey, not a destination, a journey without end. The Tendai Monks of Mount Hiei Japan take this experience to the extreme. Their Great Marathon, as they call it, is a pilgrimage of 27,000 miles! Few monks earn the honor to make this seven-year journey. One of the best known of these ultra-marathoners, Sakai, said this meditation practice "really has no beginning or end." For these "running Buddhas" this marathon was not merely a metaphor for life, it is a journey for the "good of all mankind."

In Western culture, meditation is treated as an isolated experience, and rarely integrated with the rest of life. We see "meditation" as a brief escape from the relentless daily grind of the "real world:" Maybe a half-hour on a treadmill, a long weekend at a lakeside cabin, a two-week vacation, maybe a longer sabbatical climbing Mt. Everest. In each case the objective of the "journey away" remains the same: Breaking the cycle of stress, by relaxing, having fun, and perhaps even reflecting on the meaning of life.

Zen and the Art of Motorcycle Maintenance tells of one such journey. In it Robert Pirsig goes on a pilgrimage with his teenage son, they often sit together for hours in silence: "Unless you're fond of hollering you don't make great conversation on a running cycle. Instead you spend your time being aware of things and meditating on them."

You can't help feeling you're right there, on the motorcycle riding with them, on their journey, meditating with them. You also sense that Pirsig was not only meditating on the running cycle with his son silently nestled behind him, but also when the two stopped to rest and eat, talk and sleep—and also as Pirsig replayed his feelings writing about how his pilgrimage across America took him on a journey deep into his soul.

SERENDIPITY—SYNCHRONICITY—SURPRISE!
UNPLANNED TRIPS & CHANCE MEETINGS

Perhaps because pilgrimages are by design journeys into the unknown, searching for the meaning of our lives, they often reveal unexpected secrets. After I left Morgan Stanley there was a long quiet period of soul searching in Los Angeles. For a long time Hollywood's doors were closed. Often I would just get in my car and drive, not knowing where. One day I stumbled into a retreat house in Palos Verdes. A kindly nun listened to me for over an hour.

Then she handed me a Bible and suggested I sit in the sunny courtyard and read something. *The Book of Job* flipped opened.

I'd never read it. That afternoon I read every word twice. I really identified with the guy. Job was put through hell on earth, and still had faith. Somehow, he made it okay for me to feel the way I did, confused, angry, and yet trusting in some vague Higher Power. I went on many little "pilgrimages" like that, where I had a moment of meditation with some remarkable people like that nun.

Your soul may also go into a mental space like the one motivational guru Anthony Robbins found far away on the beaches of Fiji, watching the shimmering night sky: "The quality of life changed when I went there ... I shut off all the stimulus of CNN, the million phone calls. I went deeper. I was listening to the whispers of destiny. In this environment, you don't have to try to be anything. The real you shows up." He didn't call it meditation. You don't have to. Meditation just is ... a quiet journey through life.

NINE
INTIMATE RELATIONSHIPS AS MEDITATION

My wife had a Mastermind relationship with a close friend for many years before we met. One a therapist, the other an advertising executive. In the mid-nineties she and I started our own weekly

---

The Four Rules of The New Meditation

Rule One
Focus on what you're doing this moment—*and nothing else*

Rule Two
Anything you're doing can become a meditation—*anything*

Rule Three
Trust yourself, the results are within you—*discover your way*

Rule Four
Keep it real simple, everybody meditates—*we do it naturally*

Mastermind and haven't missed since. They have run four to six hours, although an hour is more typical. And throughout the week we both feel the power of the Mastermind guiding us.

The format is constantly evolving. We open by reading from our favorite inspirational works, self-help messages and anything else that captures our spirit at the moment or addresses a particular challenge. We often have some quiet music in the background. Sometimes we'll do our Mastermind at the beach, the woods, or even an airfield watching takeoffs and landings.

We read affirmations and action plans, which we regularly update, often on the spur of the moment. We read aloud, raise questions, add suggestions, challenge each other, and ask for support. We close with prayers of gratitude.

The rules are flexible. Anything goes. We know we have an alliance, we do this in a spirit of perfect harmony, focused on a common purpose. We also know that our kind of "perfect harmony" often comes after some lengthy, tense moments struggling over some hotly contested issues ... just like any other relationship. And yet, it is meditation because we make it so!

"ONE NIGHT OF LOVE IS BETTER THAN 100,000 YEARS OF STERILE MEDITATION"

Meditation can also improve your love life as we learn in works like Miranda Shaw's *Passionate Enlightenment* and other books on Tantric Yoga. Similarly, the iconoclastic 15th century Zen Abbot and poet, Ikkyu, was quite blunt in his passion for mixing love making and meditation:

"Love play can make you immortal. The autumn breeze of a single night of love is better than a hundred thousand years of sterile meditation." Ikkyu also put love in its true context, with a poem about his little daughter: "Even among beauties she is a precious pearl; A little princess in this sorry world. She is the inevitable result of true love, And a Zen Master is no match for her."

More recently a former editor of the *Yoga Journal,* Stephan Bodian, made this delightfully titillating promise in *Meditation for Dummies:* "People who make love meditatively report greater responsiveness and more intensely satisfying, whole-body organisms

... mindful awareness helps you infuse more love into your lovemaking, allows you to connect more deeply with your partner, and can actually transform sex into a spiritual experience."

In other words, what many consider to be an indoor sport can easily be transformed into a profound spiritual experience—if you approach it as a form of moving meditation. Which proves once again that anything can be a meditation—anything—the choice is entirely up to you!

TEN
PARENTING—THE GREATEST OF ALL MEDITATIONS

When it comes to stress, nothing beats raising children. Every parent understands this. So it's no wonder family life and parenting are without question the world's number one opportunity for meditation. At its best we experience the joy of being in a moment so beautifully captured by Anna Quindlen in *A Short Guide to a Happy Life:*

"Get a life in which you pay attention to a baby as she scowls with concentration when she tries to pick up a Cherrio with her thumb and first finger. Turn off the cell phone. Turn off your regular phone, for that matter. Keep still. Be present. Get a life in which you are not alone. Find people you love, and who love you." In that relationship you will experience the ultimate meditation.

Anyone who's been a parent knows that as much as you love your kids, those moments may be fleeting. And yet, in between those "Cherrio moments" and the "you're-driving-me-crazy" stresses of dealing with a rebellious teenager, there are endless opportunities for meditation.

When it comes to raising children, parents aren't experts, we're learning on the job. We have no choice but to live in the moment! But in each of those moments you *do* have a choice.

Maybe you can't meditate like Zen or Trappist monk in a quiet monastery. And it's highly probably you'll never attain total peace and serenity around a bunch of noisy, demanding, self-centered teenagers. But you do have tools available to reduce the stress—and meditation is the best one available, even if you only get it in very brief moments—while car pooling, at a play rehearsal, making their dinner, or singing a lullaby.

Here's a message for any stressed-out parent: Ralph Waldo Emerson's definition of success. Tape it to your bathroom mirror and meditate on it when you got up in the morning: "To laugh often and much; to win the respect of intelligent people and the affection of children; to earn the appreciation of honest critics and endure the betrayal of false friends; to appreciate beauty, to find the best in others; to leave the world a bit better, whether by a healthy child, a garden patch or a redeemed social condition; to know even one has breathed easier because you have lived. This is to have succeeded."

EXPERIMENT—YOU ARE BEING GUIDED

Which zone is "the best" one for you? The Mental Zone may still be your favorite. But more likely it will be in the Sports Zone, or the Creativity Zone. And yes, often here in the Relationship Zone. Actually, in all of them, because life is a moving target and so is meditation.

Most likely you'll end up putting together an eclectic, highly personal combination you invent and customize all by yourself and for yourself, with a little of this and a little of that, adjusting on the move, depending on the time of day, the season, your life cycle, personal crises, people around you, work pressures, your precise location on the earth's surface, and so on.

The truth is, everything in life is in a state of flux, always. You stay flexible, living in the moment and open to the inevitable, the unexpected, new challenges and opportunities. And in the flow of events, the best moments will be times when the entire day was a meditation—even though you may not realize it until later, when you're filled with warm feelings of gratitude about a special relationship.

TRUST YOURSELF

You are a totally unique personality. There's nobody like you, never was, never will be. So trust your instincts. Experts and amateurs will tell what *they* think is the best way for you. Listen to them.

THE RELATIONSHIP ZONE

But in the end, you make the decision, and you live with it. Trust yourself, you will come up with the meditation program that fits you perfectly. Yes, it will take some experimenting, but that's part of the challenge, and the fun in every journey of self-discovery.

Remember The Buddha's greatest wisdom teaching: "Believe nothing, no matter where you read it or who has said it, not even if I have said it, unless it agrees with your own reason and your own common sense." Trust yourself.

More Reading about
<u>The Four Zones of Meditation</u>

THE SPORTS ZONE of MEDITATION

Art of Surfing—Raul Guisado
Be Iron Fit: Training for Triathletes—Don Fink
Bushido: The Soul of Japan—Inazo Nitobe
Chi Running—Danny Dreyer
Code of the Samurai—Thomas Cleary
Complete Book of Running—Amby Burfoot
Dancing The Wave: Mysteries of Surfing—Jean-Etienne Poirier
A Different Angle: Fly Fishing Stories by Women—Holly Morris
Fifty Places to Fly Fish Before You Die—Chris Santella
Fly Fisherman's Guide to Meaning of Life—Peter Kaminsky
Golf for Enlightenment—Deepak Chopra
Golf and the Kingdom—Michael Murphy
Golf and the Spirit—M. Scott Peck
Golfer's Book of Yoga—Drew Greenland
In The Zone—Murphy & White
The Inner Athlete—Dan Millman
The Inner Game of Golf—W. T. Gallway
The Inner Game of Tennis—W. T. Gallway
Legend of Bagger Vance—Steven Pressfield
Marathon: Ultimate Training Guide—Hal Higdon
Mastery—George Leonard
Meditation in Motion—Barbara Bartocci
The Mental Athlete—Kay Porter
Mental Game: Winning at Pressure Tennis—James Loehr
Mind Gym—Mack Casstevens
New Toughness Training for Sports—James Loehr
Overachievement—John Eliot
Path of the Warrior—Lucas Estrella Schultz
Performance Rock Climbing—Goddard & Neumann

MORE READING

Pilates, Yoga, Meditation & Stress Relief—Parragon
Real Men Do Yoga—John Capouya
Rock Climbing—Don Mellor
Sacred Hoops—Phil Jackson
The Secret Power Within—Chuck Norris
Secret Tactics—Kazumi Tabata
The Spirit of the Marathon—Gail Kislevitz
Sport Climbing—John Long
Swim Bike Run—Hobson, Campbell, Vickers
Tao of the Jump Shot—John Mahoney
Tao of Surfing—Michael Allen
Thinking Body, Dancing Mind—Chungliang Al Huang
The Ultimate Ride: Cycling—Chris Carmichael
Values of the Game—Bill Bradley
Walking Meditation—Thich Nhat Hahn
Working Out, Working Within—Lynch & Huang
The Warrior Within: Bruce Lee—John Little
The Way of the Surfer—Drew Kampion
The Way of the Peaceful Warrior—Dan Millman
The Way of Aikido—George Leonard
Zen Golf—Dr. Joseph Parent
Zen in the Martial Arts—Joe Hyams
Zen & the Way of the Sword—Winston L. King

THE CREATIVITY ZONE of MEDITATION

The Alchemy of Possibility—Carolyn Mary Kleefield
The Artist's Way—Julie Cameron
Awaken the Heroes Within—Carol Pearson
Awakening the Spirit in Everyday Life—Sam Keen
Care of the Soul—Thomas Moore
Conditioning for Dance: Peak Performance—Eric Franklin
Creative Visualization—Shakti Gawain
Drawing on the Right Side of the Brain—Betty Edwards
Handbook of Higher Consciousness—Ken Keyes
On Writing: A Memoir of the Craft—Stephen King
Rosey Grier's Needlepoint for Men—Rosey Grier
Sister Wendy's Book of Meditations—Sister Wendy
The Sound of Paper—Julia Cameron
The Writer's Life—Julia Cameron

MORE READING

The Zen of Gambling—Wayne Allyn Root
Zen & the Art of Knitting—Bernadette Murphy
Zen & the Art of Poker—Larry Phillips
Zen in the Art of Writing—Ray Bradbury
Zen Guitar—Philip Toshio Sudo

THE MENTAL ZONE of MEDITATION

Airplane Yoga—Rachel Lehmann-Haupt & Bess Abrahams
Beyond the Relaxation Response—Herbert Benson
Breakout Principle—Herbert Benson & William Proctor
Coffeebreak Pilates—Alan Herdman
Confucius Lives Next Door—T. R. Reid
Consciousness Living—Gay Hendricks
The Corporate Mystic—Hendricks & Ludeman
A Course in Miracles—Foundation for Inner Peace
Do What You Love, Money Will Follow—Marsha Sinetar
Everyday Enlightenment—Dan Millman
Flow—Mihaly Csikszentmihalyi
Fuzzy Thinking—Bart Kosko
Getting in the Gap: Meditation—Wayne W. Dyer
The Inner Game of Trading—Koppel & Abell
Journey Without Goal—Chogyam Trungpa
Money & the Meaning of Life—Jacob Needleman
Office Yoga—Darrin Zeer
Relaxation Response—Herbert Benson
Stress Management—Charlesworth & Nathan
Stress Management for the Executive—EHE Editors
Stress for Success—David Lewis
Success Through a Positive Mental Attitude—Hill & Stone
Ten Minute Stress Relief—Erica Brealey
10 Ways to Meditate—John Reps
The 20-Minute Break—Ernest Rossi
Think & Grow Rich—Napoleon Hill
The Way of Zen—Alan Watts
Zen & the Art of Making a Living—Laurence Boldt
Zen Mind, Beginner's Mind—Shunryu Suzuki
Zen at Work: in Corporate America—Les Kaye
Zenvesting—Paul Sutherland

MORE READING

THE RELATIONSHIP ZONE of MEDITATION

Fire in the Belly—Sam Keen
Healing Words—Larry Dossey
In Buddha's Kitchen—Kimberly Snow
Instructions to the Cook—Glassman & Fields
If You Meet the Buddha on the Road, Kill Him—Sheldon Kopp
Journey of Awakening: Meditators Guidebook—Ram Dass
Meetings with Remarkable Men—Gurdjieff
Passionate Enlightenment—Miranda Shaw
The Road Less Traveled—M. Scott Peck
This Thing Called You—Ernest Holmes
When Bad Things Happen to Good People—Harold Kushner
Wherever You Go There You Are—Jon Kabat-Zinn
Zen & the Art of Motorcycle Maintenance—Robert Pirsig

MEDITATION: ANCIENT & CONTEMPORARY

After the Ecstasy, the Laundry—Jack Kornfield
The Art of Doing Nothing—Veronique Vienne
The Art of Imperfection—Veronique Vienne
Awaken the Buddha Within—Lama Surya Das
The Bhagavad Gita—Ranchor Prime Translation
The Break-out Principle—Benson & Proctor
Buddhism—Steve Hagen
Chop Wood, Carry Water— New Age Journal Editors
Cultivating Sacred Space, Gardening for the Soul—E. Murray
Do You Need a Guru?— Mariana Caplan
Dr. Dean Ornish's Program for Reversing Heart Disease
Fire in The Soul—Joan Borysenko
The First & Last Freedom—Krishnamurti
Full Catastrophe Living—Jon Kabat-Zinn
How to Meditate—Lawrence LeShan
How to Practice—The Dalai Lama
I Ching Workbook—P. L. Wing
The Inner Guide Meditation—Edwin Steinbrecher
Insight Meditation—Joseph Goldstein
Learn to Relax—Mike George
Meditation—Brian L. Weiss

MORE READING

Meditation—Osho
Meditation—Monaghan & Viereck
Meditation for Busy People—Dawn Groves
Meditations—Shakti Gawain
Meditations—Marcus Aurelius
The Meditative Mind—Daniel Goleman
Memories, Dreams & Reflections—Carl G. Jung
Modern Man in Search of A Soul—Carl G. Jung
Mystics & Zen Masters—Thomas Merton
One Dharma—Joseph Goldstein
Open Mind, Open Heart—Fr. Thomas Keating
Orange Book, Meditations—Rajneesh
Personality Types—Carl G. Jung
Pocket Guide to Meditation—Alan Pritz
The Power of Myth—Joseph Campbell
The Power of Now—Eckhart Tolle
Powers of Mind—Adam Smith
The Practice of the Presence of God—Brother Lawrence
The Practice of Zen Meditation—Hugo Enomiya-Lassalle
Principles of Meditation—Simpkins & Simpkins
A Quaker Book of Wisdom—Robert L. Smith
Real Magic—Wayne Dyer
The Search: The Ten Zen Bulls—Rajneesh
Seat of the Soul—Gary Zukav
Seven Masters, One Path—John Selby
Seven Spiritual Laws of Success—Deepak Chopra
Sitting: A Guide to Buddhist Meditation—Diana St. Ruth
The Soul's Code—James Hillman
The Spirituality of Imperfection—Kurtz & Ketcham
Stages of Meditation—The Dalai Lama
Still The Mind—Alan Watts
Tao Te Ching—Lao Tzu
This Thing Called You—Ernest Holmes
The Way of Individuation—Jolande Jacobi
Your Maximum Mind—Herbert Benson

About The Author
PAUL B. FARRELL, J.D., PH.D.

Paul B. Farrell is a personal finance and investment columnist with DowJones/MarketWatch.com. He has published over 1,200 columns and frequently discusses the psychology, ethics and spirituality of money as well as practical everyday solutions. He is the author of six books, including *The Millionaire Code: 16 Paths to Wealth Building, The Lazy Person's Guide to Investing, Mutual Funds on the Net, Expert Investing on the Net,* and *The Winning Portfolio.*

Earlier Dr. Farrell was an investment banker with Morgan Stanley. He has been an executive vice president of the Financial News Network, where he was executive in charge of producing nearly a thousand hours of live cable television news; executive vice president of Mercury Entertainment Corporation, a publicly-held film production company; associate editor of the Los Angeles Herald Examiner; and executive director of the Crisis Management Group, counseling executives, entrepreneurs, politicians, healthcare professionals, athletes, rock stars, celebrities and royalty.

Dr. Farrell has four academic degrees: Juris Doctor, Masters in Regional Planning, Bachelors of Architecture, and a Doctorate in Psychology. He served in Korea with the United States Marine Corps, as a staff sergeant and aviation radar-computer technician. Today Dr. Farrell lives on the Central Coast of California with his wife, Dorothy Boyce, a psychotherapist.

www.ingramcontent.com/pod-product-compliance
Lightning Source LLC
Chambersburg PA
CBHW071453040426
42444CB00008B/1322